Financial TERRORISM

Black Money and the Indian Elite

BR LALL, IPS (Retd)

Former

Joint Director - CBI

Director General of Police, Haryana

Manas Publications

New Delhi-110002 (INDIA)

MANAS PUBLICATIONS
(Publishers, Distributors, Importers & Exporters)
4402/5-A, Ansari Road
(Opp. HDFC Bank)
Darya Ganj, New Delhi-110 002 (INDIA)
Off. ✆ 23260783, 23265523, Res. ✆ 23842660
Fax: 011-23272766
E-mail: manaspublications@vsnl.com
www.manaspublications.in

ISBN 978-81-7049-368-6
Rs. 495/-

Typeset at
Manas Publications

Printed in India at
Rajdhani Printers, Delhi
and published by Mrs Suman Lata for
Manas Publications, 4402/5-A, Ansari Road
(Opp. HDFC Bank),
Darya Ganj, New Delhi-110 002 (INDIA)

Contents

List of Abbreviations

BOT	Build Operate Transfer
BPR&D	Bureau of Police Research and Development
CM	Chief Minister
DC	Deputy Commissioner
DDA	Delhi Development Authority
DMRC	Delhi Metro Rail Corporation
DND	Delhi Noida Direct
GDP	Gross Domestic Product
HDI	Human Development Index
IIT	Indian Institute of Technology
KG Basin	Krishna Godavari Basin
MLA	Member Legislative Assembly
NCR	National Capital Region
NDA	National Democratic Alliance
NHAI	National Highway Authority of India
OECD	Organisation for Economic Cooperation and Development
PAN	Permanent Account Number
PM	Prime Minister
PWD	Public Works Department

RTI	Right To Information
Sft	Square feet
SHO	Station House Officer
Sqm	Square metre
TII	Transparency International India
UNCAC	United Nations Convention Against Corruption
VAT	Value Added Tax
Yds	Yards

Preface

Any issue that is desired to be killed, draw that into the quagmire of political polemics and be sure that it would be dumped as the nation would get tired of the spate of political wrangling and the people would regret why at all they raised it, even if the same may concern the most urgent matters of vital importance in everyday life or of lasting value, say related to the day-to-day deprivations, violations of human rights, denial of basic services like *Bijli*, *Sadak, Pani*, health of families, education of children or a host of such other issues that deeply impact the daily life of the citizen or even the security and integrity of the country. All serious issues get buried under the debris of political controversies and at the end the ordinary man finds himself worse than earlier.

The same has happened to the black money controversy. No party can take a public stance that the money should not be brought back despite the fact that those who understand the phenomenon, know full well that it is not a simple problem. Bringing back the money is very difficult, rather next to impossible in foreseeable future at least. If at all we succeed even partially, it will take decades and still any substantial success may elude. However, a positive effect of all these discussions has been that the ordinary citizen has been made aware of how systematically he has been exploited and robbed by the powers that be and how the people in power, irrespective of the political shade, have created treasures abroad.

Expectations of the people for getting their treasure back have been raised but these are not likely to be met. In due course, it will lead to great dissatisfaction and questioning of the elite and particularly when the political elite go to the people for votes. It may also lead to violence. It has become necessary to think how can we get back the money and also if there are any other alternatives to prevent the rot further.

It is possible to take solid steps so that no further black money is generated in the system, and more important, drained out abroad. The generation of black money in our economy is too high as we will see inside and everything relating to black money is so shrouded in secrecy that nothing about its magnitude or mechanism can be said with any sense of finality. The worst aspect is that it is purely an elitist phenomenon. It is these elite that have turned hostile to national interest and commit these 'crimes against humanity' as the 11th Anti-corruption Conference referred to all the corruption and black money operations. It is they who are expected to uphold and protect the national interests, but they have violated the allegiance to the country. The betrayal by the elite in this context is nothing short of treason.

Fortunately, all the political parties have been in power from time to time, so none of them can take any high moral ground as no party, while in power, ever tried to check either the black money or its siphoning abroad. On the other hand it has amply been demonstrated time and again that so far as matters relating to integrity are concerned, all the parties are guilty and so are the most of the politicians individually. Among other cases, the Jain Hawala case brought it out very clearly. Bureaucracy or the industry and business have done no better, but the basic responsibility lies with those in power, be they politicians or the bureaucrats who have betrayed the faith that the nation reposed in them. Since all are involved, so the issue is likely to be lost in the political maze.

The inspiration to attempt this book came out of the thought to present an analysis and to explore how to combat this problem, the dimensions of which are limitless. The black money is holding the economy and the ordinary citizen of the country bonded in chains.

I wish and pray for the deliverance of our economy from our own Traitor Elite who have so far been strangle holding and throttling the economy and the nation.

BR Lall

brlall@gmail.com

1

Introduction

After six decades of independence the country is still facing the same problems of lack of development, all round scarcities, and lack of infrastructure, tottering services and above all the exploitation of masses that a slave colony only faces as the object of the rulers is to use all its resources to their advantage at the cost of the natives. The fight for freedom invariably creates a strong urge to change things in our own way and in our best interests. All the policies are supposed to be oriented to that end including the development of the nation for the benefit of our people in the best possible way according to our requirements and sentiments. It is this feeling of belonging that the country belongs to us and we belong to the country that cements the bond. Such euphoria and expectations were generated in India also during the struggle for independence and intensified immediately on attainment of freedom. These were expressed by various people under various nomenclatures like Gram Rajya, Swarajya, Ram Rajya, Rashtra Nirman etc. The Indian people also saw great dreams and were prepared to strive for their realization by their devotion, dedication and self sacrifice for the nation that all the people of my generation and earlier generations (living at that time) relished in early fifties. Somehow after the independence the governance of the country could not match the expectations and within just two decades, this all yielded to a sense of despondence and 60 years later, it appears that the people have given up to dream even. In February, 2003 as Chairman of Shivalik Development Agency of Haryana I was shocked and dismayed at the aborted aspirations of the people. I was visiting a village for locating suitable site for a water storage dam in this particular village in the Shivalik Hills of Haryana. After my final approval of the site, the engineering staff set to taking measurements and working out other technical details. In the meantime I interacted with the villagers. During the conversation that focused on the condition of the people, an extremely old looking man with completely shriveled face, addressing me as Beta (son), narrated that he was about 4 years old when independence ushered in. There were unending celebrations even in their small village. He and the other children of his age could not comprehend the implications and asked the elders the meaning of *Azadi* (independence). Elders explained that now their own government would be able to develop their village as per their own needs and that they would get water. Since the endemic water shortage hit everyone, the children felt happy at the prospect. The old man, 57 years later, was in lament that "I am at the fag end of my life and would die any moment; God knows whether my son would also die as a slave or will be able to enjoy the fruits of independence" in the form of water that they had dreamt since independence but had been deprived of for the last nearly six decades. I felt guilty on behalf of the administration that was responsible for the conditions he was condemned to; so much so that he appeared like my grandfather though we were of the same age of four at the dawn of independence. Now however he also comfortably addressed me as son and I also respected his age as an old man that his appearance demanded. This is what poverty, as a result of lack of development, can lead to.

Not only by these simple villagers, but everywhere independence is seen as a turning point in self determination of our destiny but that has eluded us and we continue in the similar economic and administrative mould as in the pre-independence days. We are facing the basic problems not only of *Bijli, Sadak, Pani,* but also of lack of education, poverty and absence of all sorts of infrastructure. We fall very low on the index of human development, that too despite our immense resources. We are very high on corruption, our wealth is drained abroad and taxes are not paid by a very big chunk of our population on the incomes that accrue, or on the purchases that are made or on the goods that are produced. Collection of taxes as percentage of GDP is one of the lowest in our country in the whole world. The freedom fighters and the intellectuals at that time had regretted the flow of wealth from India to other countries. The great Hindi poet Bharatendu Harishchandra who lived from 1851 to 1886, at that time, addressed the patriots among the youth "*dhan vides chali jaat, tau jiye hot na chanchal*" (our wealth is siphoned abroad but you are not bothered). They did everything taking personal risk in that colonial era to exhort the countrymen over this great loss.

The great nationalist economist Dadabhai Naoroji alongwith some other economists propounded the drain theories to show how Indian wealth was being carted abroad. In the nineteenth century, they had forcefully opposed the drain of our national resources. Drain theories of Dadabhai Naoroji, supplemented by carefully worked out minutest details, are very well-known. Dhires Bhattacharya states, "Dadabhai himself believed that in the forty-year period between 1788-89 and 1828-29, the amount of resources transferred to Britain from India was no less than 1500 million pounds". That was quite big an amount at the price levels and the size of the economy at that time. That was the loot of the economy by the masters who plundered and carted away Indian wealth abroad, but still the process was transparent, recorded and definite, whereas today in free India, the loot is by the Indians themselves in the most clandestine way and there is no check and no effective opposition to it. The worst aspect is that a big chunk of our politicians, the bureaucrats, the business and industry alongwith mafia, are deeply entrenched in it. All these elite groups look for perks and privileges to corner more and more moolah. They do not want any laws or regulations to come in their way, though otherwise they may shout from rooftops "Be you ever so high, the law is above you".

Gandhiji had forewarned of such conditions to develop after independence so that corrective steps could be initiated well in time right in 1947 itself. He wrote as early as 1922: "We should remember that immediately on attainment of freedom our people are not going to secure happiness. As we become independent, all the defects in the system of elections, injustices, tyranny of the richer classes as also the burden of running the administration are bound to come upon us. People would begin to feel that during those days there was more justice, there was better administration, there was peace and there was honesty to a very great extent among the administrators compared to the days after independence. The only benefit of independence, however, would be that we would get rid of slavery and the blot of insult resulting therefrom." How prophetic he was and how clearly he visualised the shape of things to come. Unfortunately, our rulers failed to appreciate the prophetic words of warning from the great seer and take the corrective steps that should have been taken at the dawn of independence as was done in USA by George Washington, the first president and more recently in Singapore by its first PM in the very first year of their freedom. No wonder such nations are on a progressive path and have developed fast. They are also high on the index of integrity of the Transparency International and Human Development Index (HDI).

Not that the information or realization was lacking. Tax evasion by the high and mighty was formally brought to the notice of the powers that be by A.D. Gorwala, chairman of the committee appointed by the Government of India to look into why Indian Administration was not able to implement various programmes efficiently and effectively. In his formal report, he observed as early as 1951: "while small men are often troubled quite unnecessarily; tax-evaders, whose assessment should run into lacs, seem to escape. The failure of the Income Tax Investigation Commission to produce any real results and the ease with which the most blatant tax evaders seem to be able to manage their affairs undisturbed has caused a very widespread belief in the impotence of the government when pitted against the really influential and wealthy people." Sixty years later, only billions have replaced the lacs of that time and what is more shocking is that the tools of evasion have also been perfected.

As early as 1963 the Santhanam Committee on Corruption had noted with concern the existence of black money and its devastating effect as also the patronage to high and mighty who were virtually beyond the arm of law even at that time."We whole heartedly endorse the view that the existence of large amount of unaccounted black money is a major source of corruption..........Complaints against the highly placed in public life were not dealt with in the manner that they should have been if public confidence had to be maintained. Weakness in this respect created cynicism and the growth of the belief that while governments were against corruption they were not against corrupt individuals, if such individuals had the requisite amount of power, influence and protection."

These all were warning signals from time to time, but no cognizance was taken of any of them. Unfortunately, the same trend continues even till this day. If anything, the system of loot has been perfected. The taxes are evaded, the production is not recorded and ultimately the country is drained. During the last sixty years when immense wealth of this country was siphoned abroad, there were no protests. The ordinary people who were the affected ones resigned to their fate in helplessness.

Thank God now there is public outcry and voices are being raised to bring back the money drained so far.

It is difficult to quantify our wealth held abroad and rather impossible to have any authentic statistics as all this is shrouded under the veil of secrecy. Tax Havens are multiplying every day. During the last decade or so their number has gone up from the single digit to about six dozens though their exact number cannot be known. However a list of these slush parks as adopted by OECD is attached as Annexure "A".

A tax haven is a country or its area in part, where either there are no direct taxes or rates of such taxes are very low so that the corporate and in particular the individuals are attracted to move their income and wealth to these jurisdictions and thereby save taxes. Besides low tax rates, the successful continuation of a tax haven pre-supposes secrecy, non-sharing of any information whatsoever. Since times immemorial, the traders have been taking advantage of the differential tax rates in the neighbouring jurisdictions. In history the concept is traceable to at least 8th century. In olden times it was a marginal phenomenon relevant at the border only, but with globalization, growth of offshore banking and the ease of transfer of funds, has turned it into a general and a serious problem. No wonder that the tax havens like Cayman Island have overgrown. With as small a population as 52000, it has granted work permits to 40000 people, as many as 80000 companies/corporate have registered their headquarters in this island and 500 banks with the banking liabilities amounting to a whopping sum of $1.5 trillion in 2008 that makes it the 5th largest sector of banking, are functioning in this tiny tax haven. The island country of 264 sq km area is a wonderland cornering all this at the cost of drained nations like India. For us they are no less than thieves or terrorists who steal and deprive us of our resources.

In recent parliamentary elections, there were claims to bring back this money within 100 days. That was, no doubt, election time rhetoric as anyone with a little knowledge in such matters would know that the 100-day period is not enough even for filing the necessary application even in a single tax haven in a single case. Now that the elections are over, it needs be researched seriously what measures can be taken to bring back this wealth to this impoverished nation. This book is an effort in that direction for recovering our lost wealth, but more important is preventing the further drain abroad and improving realization of taxes so that we take care of the present and the future at least; of course the long term struggle to set the past right, can go on.

The book analyses and estimates the problem, then proceeds to examine the issue of bringing back the money and finally lays down definite steps that can prevent proliferation of black money in future by devising ways and means to check its very generation in the economy.

2

Watch, How Slush is Generated

The slush is generated via two routes. First, through the economic activity in the unaccounted sector, thereby evading all the taxes, both direct and indirect on this unrecorded GDP by hiding the whole of the economic activity and the consequential incomes generated. Ancillary to this is the income arising out of crime and exploitation that cannot be admitted. Second, by the evasion or avoidance of taxes on the incomes generated in the recorded sector. In all these cases, taxes are invariably evaded. The fact still remains that the black economy has much more than the tax evasion alone though this may be the most significant aspect. Since all this is part of utmost secrecy, any systematic analysis of other phenomenon may not be possible authentically as that of the tax evasion.

In order to prevent the tax evasion, the drain of money abroad and to look into the entire gamut of black economy as stated above, first we have to examine how do the incomes generated within the system disappear into the unaccounted stream. The production takes place in the normal course and the goods sell in the market, apparently in the normal course, but the same are not accounted or there is under accounting. This unaccounted portion is generated either by misappropriating the share of the State by pilfering and misappropriating the resources that belong to the exchequer or by not paying the taxes that may be direct or indirect like sales tax, excise duty and such other taxes. Ultimately, the income tax is also evaded on all such incomes. In the process production is not shown to have taken place at all and all payments to factors of production remain unaccounted. The goods are freely available in the market without any bills as creation of any record would disturb their applecart. Besides, the black money is also generated by misappropriating the share of others down the line by sheer exploitation.

This phenomenon can be seen in action through some illustrations by examining the cases of a few industries in order to have a feel of the process of generation of the black money in huge measures even in the insignificant industries like Beedi. Income generation in black is so normal and routine that one does not take notice of it even though its macro dimensions may be rather staggering and shocking. Let us begin with the very small industry like printing of cards for marriages.

The Card Printing Industry

The other day I had an occasion to go to Chawri Bazaar in Delhi for getting invitation cards printed for marriage of my daughter. I spent some 2 to 3 hours in the shop in checking the drafts and other such requirements. I entered into general conversation with the staff with my innocuous queries about their modernization and efficiency. That established a rapport. I made some enquiries about their working and billing and my worst fears came true. When I asked for the bill, the manager tried to dissuade me but when I insisted, he used the *RAM BAAN* that I will have to shell out four percent tax. When that also could not deter me, he opened up that not more than two percent of people would demand the bill and pay the tax. I kept on chatting and it came out that they issued fake bills on their own to bring upto of 5 percent of their business and that constituted their recorded transactions for government purposes and all their remaining business continued to be unrecorded. A rough estimate that came out of the conversation revealed that the average of their daily turnover was to the extent of Rs.1 lac. There were more than 5000 similar shops in that very market. So their daily revenue generation worked out to Rs. 50 crores, the sales tax on which amounts to Rs. 2 crores everyday, which was evaded by and large. That works out to Rs. 630 crores for the 315 working days leaving out the Sundays.

Evasion of this tax is not the only loss the exchequer suffers. When one tax is evaded, the buck does not stop there. The entire income earned goes out of the recorded stream thereby evading direct tax on the income and other indirect taxes on their own purchases are also evaded side by side. This has further far-reaching effects on the economy as the production and income accruing due to multiplier effect as chain reaction of basic income growth, all remain unrecorded. Other taxes apart, in this case there is direct loss due to non-payment of income tax on a daily turnover of Rs. 50 crores that will amount to Rs.15750 crores for the 315 working days of the year. It is well known that the margins in this business are no less than 40 percent. So the income that accrues would be of the order of Rs. 6300 crores and the income tax evaded thereon would amount to something over 1260 crores taking an average rate of taxation at 20 percent for adjustment of exemptions. There is no reason that shops dealing with other materials in Chawri Bazaar or all other wholesale and retail markets of Chandni Chowk, Nai Sarak, Fatehpuri, various Katras, Karol Bagh or other markets across Delhi would be any different. The potential of Delhi is very large as we will see in section on Black Delhi. Such concealing of income is prevalent all over the country.

Gold and Jewellery Industry

Large purchases of gold and diamonds, rather all the costly jewellery, are made in cash. Even an outlet like Tanishk, confirmed the above hypothesis in verbal discussions with the staff that 70 percent of the transactions are in cash. The firm issues all the bills/receipts etc and collects the prescribed sales tax of 1 to 2 percent, but still people prefer to carry heavy amounts in cash even at the great risk, the obvious reason is that their money is unaccounted, bill can be taken in any name. As such it is the black money that is being used. The sales tax at two percent is nominal that no one may like to evade, but since huge amounts of money for purchase of jewellery emanate from black sector, income tax on which has already been evaded, the purchaser cannot give out his real identity and as such prefers transactions in cash. The source at Tanishk informed that they insist on identity proof and PAN card number for transactions beyond Rs. 25000, but then it is well known that all these can be arranged by paying a small bribe or even by manipulating the system. Besides, splitting the bills on purchases of a single day by a single party is something usual.

To gauge the magnitude of the money involved, let us examine how much gold is imported/processed/traded in India. It is no secret that the consumption of gold is the highest in India in the whole world. The country spends a staggering amount on gold imports. Indians may go anywhere in the world, they bring back gold from there as if the destination of whole gold production of the entire world is India alone. Demand is ever rising and even the recent unprecedented steep rise in prices has made no substantial difference to demand for gold. India at present lawfully imports 1200 tons of gold.12 percent or 144 say 150 tons of this goes into the industrial use and remaining 1050 tons is processed and sold in the form of ornaments through a network of over 3.5 lacs outlets for jewellery that we are supposed to have. That gives an average of 3 kg per outlet per year, the sale proceeds of which would be worth about Rs. 45 lacs at present price level. In this industry the ostensible margins, from raw gold to the finished product, are not more than 20 percent on sale proceeds which includes the goldsmith, the jeweller, their workers and all their fixed as well as variable costs. The earnings per outlet work out to Rs. 9 lacs a year. Diamonds, pearls and silver may add another equal amount to his income from gold, raising it to Rs. 18 lacs per annum or Rs. 1.5 lac per month per outlet. Even a small goldsmith cannot defray all the charges, the staff salaries and earn a livelihood for himself on this turnover, whereas every single city has a large number of them with a retinue of employees. All the jewellers are wallowing in wealth. Obviously more gold and other valuables creep in through unaccounted sources than the World Gold Council can vouchsafe. It does not appear to be an exaggeration that the entire production of 5000 tons annual gold of the world gravitates to India through imports and smuggling in bulk as also in bits. There could not be a better proof than the case of Sheetal Mafatlal who was recently apprehended allegedly smuggling, in a most casual routine, mainly the gold jewellery worth Rs. 53 lacs single handedly in one single trip. She is said to be making many trips abroad during a year. Only God knows whether it is the story of a single trip or of every trip. As per reports in the media, she could be apprehended as some family member had tipped the customs people because of the continuing family feud, otherwise she would have gone scot free. There would be many more like her and all these are beyond the reckoning of the World Gold Council or any other agency, but it is possibly they and their likes on whom the jewellery industry heavily depends and is able to run 3.5 lac outlets. As such the exact arrivals into India would only be the guesswork, but even if it is 3000 tons, it would be worth a staggering Rs. 4.5 lac crores as against Rs. 1.8 lac crores as per the published figure of 1200 tons of World Gold Council. Besides gold, there is craze among the higher classes for the high value items like diamonds and platinum. When added to gold, the national bill for jewellery may soar to something like Rs. 7 to 8 lac crores every year of which bulk, say worth 5 lac crores could safely be funded by the black sector.

The problem has two aspects. First that the world gold trade is thriving on Indian demand that is largely a function of black money. It needs be stopped. However, our immediate problem is the Rs. 5 lac crore black money based gold market. The tax evaded on this magnitude of income @ just 15 percent (half of standard 30 percent) would amount to a minimum of Rs. 75,000 crores. This makes it clear why there is so much unrecorded or fake recorded business through cash payment for which much of gold is smuggled into the country which is paid by the black money, here, there and anywhere.

Beedi Industry

Beedi may *prima facie* seem a tiny insignificant industry, but even this is highly exploitative and generates huge black income leading to corresponding tax evasion. The conditions vary from state to state, but when I probed further, I discovered that even West Bengal, a communist ruled state that boasts of the welfare of the downtrodden, is no better in preventing generation of black money and exploitation of the simple illiterate labour. Each state has fixed its own daily minimum wage for the workers of various categories. These wage rates by themselves are quite low, but the worst is that in sectors like Beedi, the states have not been able to ensure that the labour gets even this paltry sum as per the minimum wage. It is particularly shocking that even this welfare state that apparently swears by equitable distribution of income and wealth, failed to enact and enforce the relevant laws. I was surprised to read some recent reports in media that in West Bengal, "In February 2006 the state welfare commissioner approved a pact between Beedi merchants of Murshidabad and the Beedi workers for a minimum wage of Rs.41 per thousand rolled Beedis. Experts say most workers can roll around 900 Beedis a day." The average worker thus would get Rs. 37 per day only, against the minimum wage of Rs. 64.22 per day in that state at that time. A number of ladies are also employed on this job, who even during pregnancy expose not only themselves but even the unborn child to the risk of cancer that too for Rs. 37 a day which will not suffice to provide one meal to the family. One must realize that a single simple pizza or a burger, the least costly junk food item for the middle and lower middle classes, will cost around Rs. 75, just double the daily earnings of the Beedi labourer.

The economy of Beedi making is not so bad that the labour cannot be paid the minimum wage if not the living wage. After reading the report, I studied and analysed the economy of Beedi making that presents a very interesting and very instructive account. Beedi has only two basic components, the Kendu leaf and the tobacco. After the tobacco has been rolled into the Kendu leaf as a stick, it has to be tied by a simple thread two inches long. Twenty-five Beedi sticks are wrapped into a bundle in very ordinary thin paper. The bundle is again tied with a four inch thread. Thus a bundle requires a small piece of paper and about 6 inches of thread for packing 25 Beedis. This is all that is required for a basic unit of Beedi called the bundle. Twenty bundles are again wrapped in a paper together to constitute a Pura and 48 Puras constitutes a carton. Two cartons are packed in a gunny bag containing 48,000 Beedis that weigh 25 kg. An ordinary truck carries 200 such bags weighing 5000 kg.

Though it may appear strange, but tobacco component constitutes very little cost as I opened up 100 sticks of Beedi, collected the tobacco and got it weighed from a goldsmith. It weighed just 24 gms. Taking it as 25 gms, each stick has a quarter gm and 1000 Beedis will contain 250 gms of tobacco. Price of tobacco at that time in the market was Rs. 20-60 depending upon the quality. Cigarette quality tobacco was for Rs. 35 onwards and Beedi quality fell between Rs. 20-30 per kg. Taking the higher rate of Rs. 30 per kg, 1000 Beedis required tobacco worth Rs. 7.50. The excise duty was Rs. 9 per thousand. Wrapping cost and the cost of Kendu leaf and the packing material at the most generous of the scale will not exceed Re. 1 per thousand sticks. Assuming that any Beedi produced anywhere on an average circulates upto 500 kms radius from the center of production, the average transport required would be for 250 kms, but let us take it as 500 kms so as to err on the higher side only. As per *Economic Times,* the cost of moving 9 tons of merchandise in a truck was Rs. 15 per km or Rs. 7,500 for 500 kms at that time. In this case, Beedi being a light commodity, the truck carries only 5 tons on the ground, so the amount of Rs. 7,500/- has to be paid for this tonnage. Transport cost per bag of 25 kgs will work out to Rs. 37.50. The bag with two cartons contains 48000 Beedis so the cost of transport per thousand Beedis worked out to Re. 0.78 paise. Thus the total cost of production and distribution of Beedis worked out to Rs. 59.28 per thousand as per Table 2.1 below:

Table: 2.1

Ingredients	Cost (in Rs.)
1. Tobacco	7.50
2. Kendu leaf, thread and other packing material	1.00
3. Excise Duty	9.00
4. Transport	0.78
5. Labour	41.00
Total	**59.28**
add margin of manufacturer @15 percent	68.17
add margin of wholesaler @15 percent	78.39
add margin of the retailer @15 percent	90.15

The selling price of Beedi was Rs. 5 per bundle. The 40 bundles for 1000 Beedis would have sold for Rs. 200/-. Cost of production and distribution was less than Rs. 60. Earmarking a total of 50 percent distribution margins over the cost of production, it worked out to Rs. 90 leaving out a surplus of Rs. 110 that obviously goes into the black money stream of the producer, distributor or the retailer. Since retailer in this case is a very small fry, doing very small business, the manufacturer and the distributor pocket most of the surplus. Why can't the labourers be paid a wage commensurate to the value added by them? That is the fundamental question. If the manufacturer, the wholesaler and the retailer, each is allowed 15 percent profit on his costs as calculated above, the final selling price should work out to Rs. 90.15 p only, anything over and above that amounts to the exploitation of both the labour as also the consumer, who both belong to the poorest section of the society. Finally, apart from the exploitation of labour, there is huge tax evasion and pushing of incomes into the black stream. Margins of manufacturers in this trade are very high as is borne out by the case of the Ganesh Beedi Works; Mysore. Partners of this single Beedi producing firm continued to be the highest individual taxpayers of the country. As per an article by S Kumar, that appeared in the *Illustrated Weekly of India* (now out of publication) of 16th April 1989, the seven partners of this single Beedi firm found place among the 11 highest individual taxpayers of the country for the assessment year 1988-1989. That explains the huge margin of profits in this industry that *prima facie* is very innocuous. Imagine that seven highest taxpayers of the country out of the top eleven belonged to a single honest firm called Ganesh Beedi Works. Imagine what an income Beedi industry is hiding. It is a loot of the lowest of the lowly as also of the exchequer. In all fairness and seeing the risks involved in their job of rolling Beedis, they should be entitled to the entire surplus of Rs. 110 and be paid @ Rs.150 per 1000 Beedis instead of Rs. 41 that they are getting at present. From West Bengal government that is supposed to lead, work for and protect the downtrodden, such an action is expected immediately. Maybe with improved food and health their efficiency may also go up and they may roll out more Beedis than 900.

For Industry, this sum of Rs. 110 is the black money for every thousand Beedis. When calculated at macro level, the implications are mindboggling. There were 50.53 lac Beedi workers spread over 16 states in the country. It may be a study about one state, but is by and large, equally applicable to all the other states as well. With a production of 900 Beedis per day, the total daily Beedi production in the country worked out to 454.77 crore sticks that sell for Rs. 91 crores everyday or Rs. 33215 crores annually. With a black component of Rs. 110 per thousand sticks , the total volume of black money from this non-descript industry amounts to Rs. 18257 crores and is entirely in the form of income on which the tax evaded would be about Rs. 6000 crores. The story does not end here as the three characters; the manufacturers, the distributor and the retailer avoid tax on their margin of 15 percent each. In this analysis, it has been presumed that the manufacturers pay the due excise duty. In reality it is not so and actual evasion of taxes and generation of black component would be higher still.

Corruption in Trucking Industry

In 2007 the Transparency International India conducted a survey titled "Corruption in Trucking Operations in India" in order to study the extent of corruption, its causes and proposed remedial measures. The survey had extensive coverage throughout the country. It collected statistics in details. Its focus was on the bribe amount that various agencies of the government extracted. It however, quoted useful data extensively that can be used to draw far reaching conclusions on black money generation and tax evasion. It reported that there were 44.88 lac trucks registered in the country of which about 36 lacs were in active operations. Of these 22 lacs were plying on the interstate routes and the remaining locally. The trucks on interstate routes constituted the main fleet that was responsible for the huge haulage and also for paying the hefty sum in bribes.

The study arrived at the conclusion that a truck travelled 280 to 340 kms a day or 60000 to 1,00,000 kms a year and had to shell out an amount of Rs. 0.70 paise per kilometer a truck travelled; constituting a neat sum of Rs. 79,220 as bribe to various departments during an year with major portion going for overloading. They arrived at a total figure of Rs. 22048.20 crores of bribe money paid by the truck operators to various departments of the government. Since all calculations are based on the kilometerage undertaken, it is necessary and possible to arrive at a specific figure of the same by computing the exact kilometerage from the amount of bribe money. At the rate of Re. 0.70 paise per kilometer, it will take the trucks all over the country to travel 31,497 crore kilometers to pay the amount of Rs. 22,048 crores as bribe.

The study further goes on to state that overloading between 100 and 150 percent is the rule. The bigger the truck the higher is the extent of overloading, but any basic truck with nine tonnes capacity always took a load of 15 tonnes. Incidentally Railways under Lalu Prasad Yadav (then Railway minister) were also functioning in a similar way that goods wagon authorized to carry 52 tons had a physical capacity to carry 80 tons. This excess capacity was being used by the Railway employees privately. They transported this additional baggage unofficially and pocketed the receipts for this excess capacity utilization themselves, whereas, this amount of excess receipts that they misappropriated, rightfully belonged to the Railways. Since it was government money, it amounted to corruption, but in case of truckers there is no such concept, as *prima facie* they are entitled to all these receipts as part of their business transactions. But at the same time the exchequer has been cheated in two ways. First, the fee for permit is in proportion to the authorized capacity of the vehicle. If the vehicle is approved for hauling up higher tonnage, the rates of fee for issuing permit are also higher. The state stands to lose fee to that extent, but more important is the second component that all this tonnage is hauled up unrecorded and the entire revenue and income from these operations turn black on which neither the service tax nor the income tax is paid.

On a kilometerage of 31,497 crores the implications have to be rather staggering. It is proposed to calculate the surplus/

unrecorded amount at the minimum of the rate. As per the *Economic Times* the fare rates were Rs.15-22 per kilometer for a truck with the standard capacity of nine tonnes. Taking an average of Rs.18 per kilometer for a nine tons capacity truck, the charge for 6 tons works out to Rs.12 per kilometer. The amount at this scale remains out of reckoning. There is no doubt that carrying this additional load does not cost any significant amount extra except the amount of bribe that has already been accounted for. At this rate an unrecorded amount of Rs. 3,77,964 crores is charged over a distance of 31,497 crore kilometers. Whereas the TII survey puts the overloading at 100 to 150 percent, the above figures have been worked out at 66 percent overloading that is six tons over the permissible nine tons. This at the minimum constitutes the unrecorded transactions in trucking industry even if it is presumed that all the transactions for regular capacity are accounted completely, though we very well know that it is not done. However, in the absence of any data or study no hypothesis can be made for this part.

This is a huge amount on which income tax alone works out to Rs. 1.26 lac crores as it is the additional income and upper portion of income that is subject to 30 percent slab. Moreover, all other taxes are also evaded, besides generating huge amounts of black money.

Admission to Professional Colleges

There are strange ways in our country in which the phenomenon of black money manifests itself. It plays a crucial role affecting the lives and career of youth. It is believed to have been going on since long, but the processes used to be hidden earlier, but now somehow, the same is becoming open and is being exposed. The electronic media in particular is helping a great deal by live exposures through sting operations that cannot be denied outright as it used to happen earlier. During admissions to professional colleges such as medical, engineering, management and B.Ed. colleges, naked dance of black transactions has been aired from time to time and channel to channel. Almost all the private institutes charge the capitation fee in cash for which no receipt is given. For these institutes this money remains unaccounted and unrecorded. This is over and above the official fees and the administrative charges as are ostensibly prescribed by the managements under supervision of the governments as per orders of the Supreme Court. This came to light when the TV channel "Times Now" showed a sting operation duly filmed, on the screen and focused on how actual negotiations to settle this component were taking place. The fee charged was said to vary from Rs. 20 to 75 lacs for various colleges for different categories of candidates for admission to MBBS. Barring some new colleges that charged Rs. 20-30 lacs, most of the colleges are supposed to be charging Rs. 40 lacs onwards going upto 75 lacs for NRI's. As the rates appeared to be rather diabolical, it prompted me to conduct a little research and work out total black money countrywide for launching a career in this noblest of all the professions. The table below lists in column 2 the average rates that are being charged in the private institutions all over the country. Column 3 shows the number of seats available in private institutions and column 4 gives the overall implications of money if all the seats are charged at these minimum average rates.

Table 2.2: Number of Seats and Rates of Capitation Fee

Name of the course	Rate of Capitation Fee (In lacs)	No. of Seats in private colleges	Financial Implications (In crores of Rs.)
1	2	3	4
MBBS	40	17020	6808
BDS	15	19960	2984
MD/MS	150	500	750
P.G.in Radiology	200	100	200
TOTAL			10742

A whopping Rs.10,000 crores is unimaginable, but real. There may be some negligible downward revision as they may not be able to charge for 100 percent seats. But that will only be nominal and would not disturb the conclusions reached above. How unfortunate that our budding professionals commence their career in such dismal circumstances. In profession, they start collecting their investment but then the greed takes over and our professionals remain unscrupulous all through their lives, some exceptions, of course, shine apart. I studied only the medical profession and not the engineering and others which are also subject to similar black money operations, but the story in a nutshell is very clear that if the black money involved for all the other professions combined ,is taken equivalent to the medical profession, the extent of black money in admissions would amount to no less than Rs. 20,000 crores every year which is paid in cash mostly out of black income but even if some people pay out of recorded income, all such money gets turned into slush once it goes into such hands.

Apart from professional institutions, there is big money involved by way of donations, even in school admissions in most of the private schools i.e. other than the government schools. However that cannot be assessed in the absence of any reliable data, but since the number of students seeking admission at school level is large, so the financial implications will also be proportionately very high.

Construction Industry

Construction is perhaps the biggest single industry in the country after agriculture. It is not only big in size but also is the blackest of all, so much so that its exact size is also a matter of debate with different estimates showing wide variations from 6.5 to 15.7 percent of the GDP. Exact figures could be known about public sector, but not the private sector, where bulk of the investment is in black money. However, so far as the role of black money is concerned, strange though it may seem, it plays a crucial role even in public sector. Public sector awards works for execution to the contractors and it is they who make purchases of construction material from the market. Their purchases, by and large, are in cash evading all the taxes as far as possible. No wonder, despite the belief that a very substantial part of this industry is in public sector, most of the purchases even for public sector are made in the black market.

For long, this industry was believed to contribute 6.3 of the GDP, but Argudadeep and CVR Murthy of IIT Kanpur quote Swarup and Mahajan placing the size of the industry in 2001 at three lac crores contributing 15.7 percent of the GDP. In between most other estimates place it at 8.5 percent, though the Indo-Italian Chamber of Commerce and Industry places its size at 11 percent. These variations have to be there in a sector substantially fed from the black channels, depending upon what portion of black sector has been taken into account in a particular estimate. Further, the statistics about the industry are distorted from two sides. The private sector depresses the costs in order to conceal the utilization of black money and in public sector costs are inflated in order to corner a part as hush money and that precisely leads to generation of black money in the public sector itself. This aspect was highlighted by Satyendra Dubey in the context of the National Highway Authority of India (NHAI)as will be seen in details a little later.

There is another cardinal way to look at the size of the industry. The labour employed by this sector is 3.2 crore persons. At an average wage rate of Rs.100 per day for 300 days in an year, the total wage bill, by itself, will work out to Rs. 96000 crores, whereas 8.5 percent of GDP in 2001 would amount to a total of Rs. 1.62 lac crores only. Out of total investment of this order, the share of wages cannot be Rs. 96000 crores as share of labour is considered at 20-25 percent of the total expenditure in the construction industry. So the estimates by Sarup and Mahajan appear to be more near the reality. This will place the construction industry at Rs. 7.4 lac crores for 2007-08. However, even if we adopt a figure of 12.1 percent falling in the middle of 8.5 and 15.7 percent, the size of the industry in 2007-08 would still be of the order of Rs. 5.7 lac crores.

The dark side of this industry came authentically in public view with expositions by Satyendra Dubey. Fired with zeal to serve the nation with a mission, the young IIT graduate spurned the cushy jobs and joined NHAI. He protested against the practice of inflating the estimates by 40 percent at the initial stages and ultimately drawing it from the exchequer by bills, the authenticity of which could not be vouchsafed truthfully. When his struggle in the field was opposed by all, he addressed a letter to the then PM detailing the mechanism and the extent of bungling. When his letter was still circulating the bureaucratic meanders, the information leaked and he was murdered supposedly by the interested groups. A copy of his letter appears as Annexure "B". In his letter he had expressed apprehension to his life and requested for keeping it secret, but still it leaked. One would have expected the country to wake up after his supreme sacrifice, take action on what he had written, but nothing happened and things have settled back to the same routine. Formal tributes are paid to him every year, but what he stood and died for has completely been forgotten or perhaps ignored and the rates continue to rule high. My own experience having worked in this industry for full seven years confirms what Satyendra Dubey had stated. Unlike him, I was at the head of an organization and could enforce the standards with iron hand and could cut down the costs by 35-40 percent as compared to earlier. At the same time State PWD continued to pay 40 to 50 percent higher than the corporation that I was heading.

This sector covers whole of the length and breadth of the country both in government as well in the private sector. With emphasis on infrastructure, public sector, of late, has rather been expanding fast. So, the formation of black money and evasion of taxes has also been growing correspondingly. It has now been well established as above, that 40 percent of the estimated amount in public sector is never invested and bogus bills that are not subject to taxes are filed. Out of the remaining, no taxes are practically paid on purchase of material by the contractors/sub-contractors/petty contractors.

I conducted extensive survey during the last few months and it transpired that the tax evasion is general on purchases of material in building industry. All the shopkeepers had the same story to tell that sales against bill i.e. the recorded sales were only 5 to 7 percent and if it reached 10 percent, the average was considered to be very high. I asked for the bill from one shopkeeper from whom I had purchased some building material. He stated that I will have to shell out tax in that case. I got angry, rebuked him and took him to task how could he think of me as a thief who will steal the tax. He was shaken to the core, and then confessed that customers normally were not prepared to pay tax. I accused him of enticing the customers as in my own case, but he had his own story that at the end of the month they sit and issue bills to bring their recorded sales to 10 percent of the actual, for consumption of Sales Tax and Income Tax departments and pay tax on the balance out of their pocket. He further remonstrated that they can never flaunt their affluence. Though their household expenditure in the joint family was Rs.10,000 a day or Rs. 3 lacs in a month, their declared income for the entire family was Rs.10,000 PM. To the natural question that how they managed, in particular, the four vehicles that he had told remained at home and that have to be on record, other things of course may be easy to manage. His explanation was plain and simple that all the vehicles were in the name of the firm and all the journeys whether personal or official were accounted as official. Even other household expenses that could be booked against the firm were so booked, though the household and the other expenses were ordinarily transacted in cash drawn out of the black money stream. The citizen building the house by and large avoids paying tax even on patent items like steel and cement. Unfortunately, all the items are available in the market for cash purchase without paying the VAT. I have never been able to understand if excise duty is paid on all these products then how these move out of the accounted stream, but the fact on the ground is that all the materials are available on cash, evading the sales tax. God knows what happens to excise duty whether it is paid or not , but one thing is certain that in addition to sales tax, the income tax is also evaded. In private sector constructions, skipping bills in purchases is general; thereby evading VAT immediately and other taxes ultimately. *Prima facie* there appears to be no way to check this evasion individually. The cost of construction in private by individuals, as declared are normally about 25 percent of the actual unless the construction is with bank loan or there is any other such reason.

The experts put the cost of material purchased in building industry at 40 to 60 percent of the total, depending upon the nature of the work and the executing agency. Labour and equipment costs another 20 to 30 percent and the remaining is for supervision, profits and overheads. So, in a fair system, a minimum of 50 percent of total expenditure in the construction industry, on the average should be subject to VAT and other taxes that are evaded. In 2007-08 layout of construction sector as worked out earlier was at least Rs. 5.7 lac crores. As per analysis above, the expenditure on material purchased comes to Rs. 2.85 lac crores. The loss to exchequer on account of VAT alone would be of Rs. 25,000 crores at the minimum, apart from the other taxes like the income tax excise duty etc. If the evasion of other taxes is taken equivalent to the loss on account of VAT, the total tax loss rises to over Rs. 50000 crores.

The Builder Phenomenon

It is a well known fact that there is terrible shortage of residential units in the country. Till eighties the individual would purchase a plot and construct a house on his own. A small plot of land was within the reach of the middle and even the lower middle classes. Even below them could afford smaller plots measuring 25 syd. In eighties, the big builders started entering the housing market by acquiring vast tracts of land to be colonized in future. The prices of colonized land started rising and soared very high in the nineties and in the current decade these absolutely skyrocketed. As land prices soared, purchasing even a small plot became difficult and the flat culture ushered in the metropolitan cities and in no time gained popular acceptance. Earlier it had existed in a few big cities like Mumbai, Delhi etc. but now in view of high prices of land, it has been well received in other smaller cities as well. Though flat culture had come to Delhi a decade or two earlier but most of the flats at that time were four storeyed only. The high-rise culture came to Delhi in eighties only. With high-rise culture where small piece of land is to be shared by many, the builder and the cooperative societies became relevant and the builder stole over the societies in due course. The allotment of land from state agencies/cooperative societies was not an easy task in view of the rampant corruption and this very reason not only made things easier for the builders but also helped them. Further, the builders purchased large chunks of land on their own and started colonizing mainly by constructing flats. Cooperative society being a small unit and bound by the rules, could neither afford to purchase large chunks of land, nor could be permitted to enter the open market; so they depended mainly on the state agencies that were not cooperating for the obvious reasons of corruption. It was also a general belief in public that the builder mafia by bribing the officials of state agencies had restrained them from allotting plots to cooperative societies as per their requirements, with the result that in a town like Gurgaon 30,000 societies were bidding for just 33 plots in 2006. That indicates the difference between demand and supply and it is on this difference that the builder played upon and cornered money literally by tons.

As it is, the land cost per sft in case of flats works out very low. Taking the case of Gurgaon, the millennium city, the societies were allotted land at Rs. 4,000 per sqm making for 1.6 crores per acre that can support almost one lac sft of saleable/chargeable area. So the land cost was only Rs. 160 per sft for the societies. For the builder, however, it would be much less as he purchases land in bulk directly and secondly his cost of development is much lower as compared to the corruption ridden government agencies. It all goes to his profits.

Considering the costs of the private builder, first his purchase of land is at very economic rates. As the state initiates steps to acquire land in a particular location, the builders enter and purchase the land in the neighbourhood by offering a little higher price. They ascertain the plans in advance through their influence as also through corrupt practices and enter even before the state agencies enter that area. They park their black money or the deposits collected from the applicants and acquire vast chunks of land for being colonized at future dates. For bulk of the constructed areas sold in recent past, the lands in Gurgaon were purchased at a rate of Rs. 2 to 5 lacs per acre. The statutory fees as also the development costs, all combined, would not exceed Rs. 10 to 15 lacs per acre at the most generous estimates. That constitutes a total of Rs. 20 lacs for one lac sft of covered area in an acre or Rs. 20 per sft. The cost of construction of general specifications at that time for the high-rise buildings was not more than Rs. 600 to 700 per sft, whereas no builder in Gurgaon sold any flat at that time for less than Rs. 1500 to 1700 per sft creating huge margins for black money. What is true for Gurgaon holds equally good for any other place. The customers and the government were taken in, as they believed that all the transactions were in white but they didn't realize that whosoever offered, the black money was entertained readily. It is difficult to believe how black money could be accepted on advertised prices at which they were selling and issuing receipts. The mechanism followed was rather simple that the flat will be booked at the full advertised amount and then discount equal to the cash component would be allowed. Apart from above, the normal ways to create black money by filing false bills as also the inflated bills cornering as much money as they feel, are generally adopted. This all creates a huge reserve of black money around and wherever builders have gone, black money has travelled with them.

The cooperation of governments is sometimes absolutely marvelous in generating and cornering the black money. I observed this aspect when there was talk of development of land of Dharavi slum in Mumbai through the private builders. Dharavi, the biggest slum of Mumbai, which some claim to be the biggest slum of the world, covers an area of 557 acres on which the authorized floor area that could be constructed at that time, was 7 crore sft. A duly constructed flat of 224 sft was proposed to be given to each of the slum dweller who is the actual present occupants of the land. This will cover a total area of 1.2 crore sft. Another 70 lac sft was earmarked for the common services like schools, markets, hospitals etc and the rest 5 crore sft was proposed to be handed over to the private builders. They were to develop this 2 crore sft area, construct flats and the community service areas at their own cost and hand it over to the slum dwellers free of cost. The remaining land with the permissible area of 5 crore sft was to be placed at the disposal of the developers to be utilized by them and sold in the market on their own at prices to be determined by them only. The two crores sft area that they had to develop, construct and transfer free, would have cost no more than Rs. 2,000 crores at a rate of Rs. 1,000 per sft. That they get five crore sft area for just 2,000 crores or their land cost per sft was only Rs. 4. Their investment of Rs. 2000 crores will be set off by allotting them just a little over one lac sft of floor area. The other 4.99 crore sft of floor area was all bonanza.

The slum dwellers were given a raw deal by allotting them just 224 sft per family unit. This small area does not provide adequate living space for any family howsoever small. Second, they deserved better treatment, as it is they who had made such a big chunk of land available. Why couldn't they be provided with a livable flat of at least 500 sft? State should have kept their interest at the top and not those of the builders' lobby.

The builders' lobby would have mopped up anything between Rs. 2 and 5 lac crores as this author pointed out in his write up that appeared in the *Pioneer* of Delhi. The article titled "Don't handover Dharavi on a platter for a song" is attached as Annexure-"C". The base price in the far flung areas of Mumbai was Rs. 17000 per sft, though in the central/posh areas the rates were upto Rs. 1.4 lac per sft. Five crore sft area in Central Mumbai facing the sea was capable of being sold at an average rate of 1.2 lac per sft for a total of Rs. 6 lac crores. Actually more could be expected as part of the area was to turn commercial. The cost of development and construction would not exceed one lac crores in any circumstance. Thus Rs. 5 lac crore will be the neat earning of the builders and that is my immediate concern as it will lead to generation of a huge mound of black money with the builders I cannot hazard any guess how much black money will be generated but it will lie somewhere between Rs. 3 and 5 lac crores . That will cause a chaos and create unimaginable inequalities in the society that too not through economic forces, but through sheer corrupt practices that will have repercussions not only for Mumbai but the whole of the country.

The above instance is from Mumbai but is applicable *mutatis mutandis* to the whole of the country. This area generates perhaps maximum of black money as most of the transactions are in cash. This phenomenon will also be illustrated in the next section as well.

The Registration of Property

Land registry anywhere in the country is a big scandal point where scams and bungling are executed day in and day out. First, the deeds are registered at much lower a rate than those prevailing in the market. Second, even for that rate the whole payment is not insisted through banking instruments. A part is paid in cash and is only declared as paid/accepted before the authority. Third, the registering authority mostly charges one percent extra in cash, ostensibly to defray the expenses that he has to incur on behalf of his seniors i.e. deputy commissioner etc. as the registrar will ordinarily like the people to believe. That also includes the expenditure on the hospitality of the visiting dignitaries and also to provide to district officers such other things as are not approved by the government but are desired by them. Air conditioners and mobile phones fall in this category. There could be many more items. So much is for the officers who are classed as honest. The registering officer who is normally a tehsildar also takes care of the household and other needs of the DC in particular, if the latter so desires.

I am tempted to narrate a particular instance in the context of the registry. I was SP in a district after my return from deputation to the Government of India. It was practically my first district posting as SP, though technically I had been posted SP some five years earlier to that, but soon issues cropped up between me and the home minister as also between a brother and a sister of the CM who were located in my district, which otherwise was insignificant and peaceful. The home minister wanted me to play politics which I firmly declined and that was the proverbial last straw on the camel's back and I was transferred just after five weeks of taking over.

Five years later I returned to the second district. The then CM was visiting the district on that particular day. He was in his personal drawing room attached to his bedroom. As I entered the Rest House, an MLA wanted to have a word with me. So we entered the general drawing room. I was surprised to see some 30-40 tea packs of a kg each, two standard one quintal bags of sugar, a huge pile of biscuit packets and some other sundry items. Enquiries from the Tehsildar and the SHO standing in that room were futile as both remained tight lipped. Later the SHO confided that whenever CM visited, lots of such things were collected like that and subsequently these were transferred to the residence of the DC as he received lots of guests whom he had to entertain. That, the Tehsildar made all the arrangements for which he collected one percent of the registration fee unofficially, in addition to the official charges. The SHO apologized for remaining quiet on that day as the Tehsildar was also present there. From that day onwards except water, I never took anything in the Rest House or any of the state functions organized in the district.

Reverting to the property registry, it is perhaps the biggest creator and consumer of the black money. Since the amount for which the land and the buildings are registered have no relation with their market price, the administration has resorted to the concept of circle rates prescribing the minimum rates for a particular area at which a registration deed would be executed. But even these rates have no semblance with the prevailing market rates. The circle rate could be anywhere between 5 to 25 percent only of the real value as is apparent from the Tables 2.3 and 2.4 below showing comparable market rates and the circle rates of various areas for the state of Delhi. This is the problem all over the country, but is most serious in all the metros.

Table: 2.3

Name of area	Market rate per syd (In lacs of Rs.)	Name of area	Market rate per sqd (In lacs of Rs.)
Prithvi Raj Road/Aurangzeb Road	3.5 to 4.0	Panchsheel Anand Lok	3.7 to 4.0
Chankya Puri	6.5 to 7.0	Niti Bagh SDA	2.7 to 3.0
Golf Links Jor Bagh Sunder Nagar	6.5 to 6.7	Friends Colony Maharani Bagh	2.5 to 2.7
Shanti Niketan/West End	4.8 to 5.0	Greater Kailash I&II	2.4 to 2.6
Vasant Vihar Anand Niketan	4.0 to 4.2		

Market rates have been taken from the weekly *Times Property* dated 15 August 2009 who in turn have quoted from CB Richard Ellis. To check malpractices and undervaluation the government has devised the concept of circle rates. These are the minimum rates below which no registration deed would be executed. The order of 2007 divides various localities of Delhi into eight categories, A to H depending upon the prevailing market rates as perceived by the official machinery. The category wise rates are listed in Table 2.4 below.

Table: 2.4

Category	Rates per Sqd	Category	Rate per Sqd
A	Rs. 43000	E	Rs. 18400
B	Rs. 34100	F	Rs. 16100
C	Rs. 27300	G	Rs. 13700
D	Rs. 21800	H	Rs. 6900

Even the highest rates bear no semblance to the lowest market rates listed above as the highest rates in the *Times Property* are 16 times the highest circle rates. Since these rates are open, then why the government cannot bring the circle rates at par with the market rates or at least near to them. Further, even these moderate rates are attracted to only few localities as out of 2025 localities or the circles of Delhi that have been enumerated in the relevant notification of Delhi government, only 24 fall in A category and 47 in B and all others are in lower categories with abysmally low rates. Assuming that the rates would be in the same proportion in every category, the market price of land is 16 times the circle rate or the government gets only six percent of its real due.

Just to test check, on a Saturday when supplements for properties are inserted in the newspapers, I rang up some 20 property dealers in Delhi/Gurgaon posing as a purchaser of the bungalow, flat or the builders' floor as the case may be. Over the telephone, I bargained for minimum amount in white as they call it at which the registration would be done and almost every single builder/property dealer agreed for 20-25 percent consideration through cheque/draft and the remaining 75-80 percent in black as unrecorded. The market value for flats and floors here works out to 5 times the circle rates. The logic is simple that the rates for construction as notified are nearer to market rates and input of land in case of a flat or a floor is low, so the ratio gets depressed. The ratio in case of land area remains the same around 16 times as seen above.

There is no reason why the things should be different anywhere else in the country except slight local variations here or there. In smaller places where no circle rates have been prescribed the conditions can be expected to be much worse.

The loss to the exchequer is twofold. First, the loss of the registration fee and the other that of the income tax. A general complaint is that the rates of registration at 6 to 8 percent are too high and the registrars charge another one percent over and above that, as hush money. All that deters the prospective buyers who in turn save something and balance the loss by under-registration. Once having been tipped, the state apparatus also helps them in the process. The rates of registration fee were lowered sometime back but were again raised as the collections had fallen down. This is the general pattern of taxation in the country that for the sins of the thieves who are the tax evaders and the unscrupulous public servants, the tax rates are hiked further, punishing the honest tax payer. There is urgent need to bring down these rates and to do away with the share/tip of the registrar. The state as a whole loses much more on income tax @ 30 percent. All out efforts be geared to bring higher and higher portion of the transactions to the recorded fold. The government should raise the circle rates steeply, but lower the rate of registration fee and bring it to 2-3 percent only so that there is incentive for more and more of payments in white and the exchequer collects more as income tax and still more important is that more and more economy moves into the accounted sector.

Infrastructure Building

All the infrastructure works have tremendous potential to generate black money and also capacity to hide all the slush. It may be the work of laying a Railway line, constructing an airport, a power plant, a village road or a national highway. Any number of examples could be quoted from any of the sectors. It is proposed to cite an actual illustration from the national highway sector where a brilliant engineer had to sacrifice his life for exposing the loot.

Satyendra Dubey, an alumnus of IIT Kanpur, was selected for civil services at a fairly high merit but chose to continue in Engineering service. He had the guts to expose the system and take it headlong. He brought out and wrote to the then PM in 2002 that there was complete bungling in the Rs. 54000 crore National Highways construction programme. He submitted that the mischief started with the selection of contractors and continued through the appointment of supervisors and consultants, in awarding very liberally the mobilization advance. Works were sublet against the laid down norms and the bidder contractors acted only as the commission agents who pocketed 40 percent of the contract value and walked away. Since he had hit where it hurt the most, the contractors as also the authorities feared being exposed, Satyendra was murdered. Though he left everything in black and white about the NHAI, but nothing has happened. He had written during the regime of NDA that changed long back. The political shade makes no difference to the attitudes of governments towards corruption. The same rates continue and have rather been revised further in due course. He, as site engineer left firsthand account that there was a play of 40 percent in the estimates and the rates at which the works were being awarded.

That is the sample story. As mentioned elsewhere, my personal experience of working in an engineering department in Haryana is identical to that and so is also my experience in CBI by observing various departments of the Government of India. I state even at the risk of repetition that in Haryana I could bring the rates of construction down by 35-40 percent and the works were executed in the corporation that I headed at almost half the rates as compared to PWD and almost all the other departments of the government.

Whereas the social costs of road building to this country should be hardly anything in comparison to what we actually incur. The labour costs are rock-bottom low and stone, the basic raw material comes free to our country. The only cost is that of mining i.e. nominal and the transport. Transport costs are also very low as this resource is available all over the country. Contrast with Netherland that is supposed to have one of the best roads in the world, but it has no stone whatsoever. It imports stone from the neighbouring countries from an average distance of 800 kms. It is transported to the port of the exporting country through rail or road and then it is loaded into the ship that carries it to their own coast, where again it has to be carried by rail or road to the place of use. Not only their transport costs are very high, they have also to pay for the material. In India the only costly item in road building is the bitumen or the cement depending upon what material is used. We have traditionally been using the bitumen, an imported item as against the cement that can be manufactured within the country. Limestone, the basic and the bulk ingredient for cement is also amply available in the country and like the other stone this is also a free gift of nature, but cost of cement has also been pegged very high by the cartels. However, now progressively we are diverting to concrete roads. But costs continue to be very high.

The answer lies in the corruption and the black economy. Satyendra Dubey pointed to 40 percent inbuilt play. As an engineer, he rightly took market prices of inputs as given, but in view of the discussion in the foregoing paragraph, the real cost of road building to this nation should not be more than 25 to 30 percent of what is being charged at present.

The BOT (Build, Operate and Transfer) projects are the worst possible. Besides executing at higher rates, much more is collected on the BOT Toll Plazas. The National Highway Authority of India (NHAI) is constructing highways and expressways on the principle of BOT for which toll fee is levied on the users for a period of 20-30 years from the time of allotment of the work. The rate of collection of toll is so high and for such a long period that it has no relation or relevance with the expenditure incurred. Delhi Gurgaon Express Highway along with its flyovers has been completed at a cost of Rs. 701.62 crores. The private agency has been given rights to collect toll at three points namely km 14 (IGI Airport) km 24 (Gurgaon Delhi border) and km 42 (Kherkidaula) plazas for a period of 20 years from January 2003 (collection to commence on completion of construction) upto January 2022. The entire amount is to be retained by the builder upto the traffic volume of 1.30 lac vehicles for each plaza beyond which the revenue has to be shared with the NHAI. The rates of toll prescribed initially w.e.f. February 2008 on this stretch are given below in Table 2.5.

Table: 2.5

Rates at Toll Plaza at

	Km 14	Km 24	Km 42
Bus/Truck/ MAV (in Rs.)	34	51	64
Minibus/ LCV (in Rs.)	17	25	32
Car (in Rs.)	11	17	21

The rates are to be reviewed annually w.e.f 1st April every year based on the wholesale price index. The due revisions have already occurred twice.

The daily collections as per the media reports averaged between Rs. 70 lacs and 1 crore a day or upto Rs. 365 crores a year at the commencement of collections in January /February 2008. As per the figures supplied by the NHAI based on the statement of the tolling firm, the collections at km 14 and km 42 were over 10 crores a month initially or 130 crores a year, but the Authority did not give out the statistics for the third barrier at km 24. However, the inference is clear from the number of collection points put up at each barrier that puts the traffic volume at km 24 easily more than the aggregate at the other two places. Safely, the total collections will work out to Rs. 22 crores per month for February-March 2008 and with 13 percent increase in rates on 1st April 2008, the figures rise to Rs. 293.8 crores per annum. In further analysis for the sake of simplicity, I propose to ignore the collections that the firm made in two months of February and March 2008.

The two factors that determine the collections are the number of vehicles that is ever rising and the rate per vehicle which is to be revised annually. In 2008 between January and April the rates witnessed an upward revision of over 13 percent and the number of vehicles on these points has been rising much faster than the available estimated rate of 9 percent. These estimates are not very reliable as the vehicle population in recent past in Delhi has seen a rise of 15 percent and in Gurgaon 25 percent. So the number of vehicles plying on this stretch should go up by 20 percent, but in the absence of any authentic assessment, even if we adopt the old conservative projected rate of 9 percent, the total collections on both counts together will see an annual rise of 22 percent. This rate of increase in annual collection has been adopted in Table 2.6 below.

The total investment on the project was Rs. 701.62 crores. The firm has to be paid only interest over and above this investment and nothing more. From the table below it is clear that even if a very high interest @ 18 percent per annum is allowed, in less than three years, the entire amount with interest would stand paid, leaving a surplus of Rs. 116.55 crores and the barriers should disappear thereafter.

Table 2.6 Statement of Annual Payments and Balance

(In crores of rupees)

Uptil March 2008	Outstanding	Annual interest	Total	Recovery	Balance
2008-09	701.62	126.29	827.91	293.80	534.11
2009-10	534.11	96.14	630.25	358.44	271.81
2010-11	271.81	48.93	320.74	437.30	- 116.55
Total					**1089.54**

There should be no need for any more payments and hence any more collections after three years, but the agreement authorizes the firm to collect Toll for 15 years upto 2022-23 if it is not extended beyond that. At the enhanced rate of fee and the rapidly growing traffic volumes, the collection for the remaining 12 years will add to a whopping sum of Rs. 23,290 crores.

The collections at the same annual rate of growth as above worked out for the next 12 years are listed in Table 2.7.

Table 2.7: Collections for remaining period of the concession

Year	Collections
2011-12	533.50
2012-13	650.87
2013-14	794.07
2014-15	968.76
2015-16	1145.29
2016-17	1397.25
2017-18	1704.64
2018-19	2079.67
2019-20	2537.19
2020-21	3095.37
2021-22	3776.37
2022-23	4607.16
Total	23290.13

Allowing any collections beyond three years would tantamount to robbing the road users and it would further escalate if actual collections were more than Rs. 293.80 crores during 2008 (on the basis of which all other figures have been arrived at), or number of vehicles rises faster or if wholesale price index escalates faster.

Does it appeal to reason that against Rs. 700 crores of investment the nation should pay over Rs. 24,000 crores? If such are the rates, it will be better that Government make lump sum payment to the contractor by levying a further cess of a rupee or two on every litre of petrol/diesel sold in the NCR to defray these expenses. Incidentally the entire amount would stand paid in three years for all the toll points that function in this area including DND, the Gurgaon-Express Highway and all others

The assumptions and the criteria that form the basis of determining the rates and the time period at Toll Plaza need intense scrutiny for all the 20 odd projects under BOT category all over the country. Detailed information had been asked for through the RTI route, but as usual there is tendency to conceal more than communicate, as the departments feel threatened in informing the citizen for fear of being exposed. The citizen naturally and rightly smells rat and wonders why there should be such grave fear from information becoming public if they do not have any bungling to hide.

The information received in response to the application under RTI, makes two rather surprising revelations. First, that "The rates......are being revised for every year starting from 1st April on the basis of wholesale price index" and secondly "the fee shall be collected in perpetuity by the Central Government." It is not understood, what is the link between a payment that has been frozen after the construction and the future price index. Further how and why can even the Government go on collecting huge money in perpetuity when it is a fee and not a tax?

The rules covering the agreement provide for all sorts of escalations but are silent on the annual count of vehicles. The way the traffic volume is rising on this road, the count should be a monthly exercise. Now at least a onetime census for counting the number of vehicles by some neutral agency, in association with some members from civil society, is very necessary in order to know the exact dimensions as the estimated base number as also the rate of increase of the vehicle population assumed at 9 percent, has been left far behind. Experts informally confided that the number of vehicles at km 24 alone was over 2 lacs in place of 1.4 lacs being quoted generally in state briefings.

The most serious aspect, with which we are concerned immediately, is the creation of black money, evasion of taxes and the resultant further loss of incomes that accrue through the multiplier effect and the further cumulative loss of taxes. Bulk of the surplus of Rs. 23,290 crores will be disposed of in many ways. First of all, the receipts at the windows will not be shown in full. Secondly, lots more people will be shown as working and drawing salary that will go to the pocket of the builder. It has happend in case of a firm like Satyam that salary for 10,000 non-existing employees used to be remitted to USA and received by the men of Ramalingam there. Further, there are many more ways to show fake expenses and evade taxes on the same. The state and the society will not only lose the tax, but also suffer drain of the accumulated black money, part of which will surely find its way into the secret accounts of the foreign banks in the tax havens.

It may not be possible to check the above fully, but there are ways and means to contain it. Satyendra Dubey in his letter of 2002 (annexure B) has discussed how to prevent 40 percent extra in building of National Highways. That leaves Gurgaon Express Highway, a project of only Rs. 420 crores, against which the nation is made to pay as high as Rs. 24000 crores. What a pity? At this rate getting works executed under BOT is not worth. It is a prolonged curse. Total works on highways executed both by the NHAI and the Surface Transport Ministry including under BOT, are worth Rs. 20,000 crores for 2008-09. If another rupee is levied as cess on the petroleum products, that will yield an additional amount of Rs. 8000 crores raising the total to Rs. 24,000 crores, more than sufficient to cover the whole of the annual expenditure during the year and still leave out some surplus, rendering all the collections all over the country irrelevant. The expenditure may increase in future but so shall also the petroleum consumption that will automatically push up the revenue on this count. That will eliminate the need for Toll barriers altogether and remove the irritants at so many places for all times to come.

It can be looked from another angle as well. The total expenditure of NHAI on its 15-year programme is projected as Rs. 2,20,000 crores. The average annual expenditure works out to less than Rs. 15,000 crores per year. As against that the petroleum cess after raising its rate by another rupee for the entire country, will yield more than the annual expenditure. So, where is the need for barriers? Moreover if payments are made side by side, many more firms will be able to undertake and participate in the process. That will certainly bring the rates steeply down to the competitive levels.

It was really surprising when the new Surface Transport Minister Kamal Nath immediately after taking over made a startling statement that for many projects none had offered to bid as the rates in BOT projects were not attractive to the contracting firms. This is in sheer contrast to what Sateyender Dubey had strove and died for. It is also directly opposite to our findings above. To understand why firms are not coming forward, one has to go a little deeper into the working of the system that permits only the big firms to bid and there are very few big firms that are eligible to bid. All others are eliminated in the peculiar conditions that are prescribed for determining the eligibility. These conditions are worked out in a way that most of the firms are automatically rendered ineligible, leaving only the desired ones in the field. Thus NHAI has zeroed down only a few big contractors who only are able to bid. They form cartels and make offers according to the rates agreed among themselves. These firms act more like commission agents that get the works allotted and further distribute the same for execution to many sub-contractors and the petty contractors. They themselves walk away with a hefty sum that Satyendra Dubey put at 40 percent. As he depicted, the worst is that it happens with the blessings from the officials. Rates naturally go high. The real competition has to be generated by allowing smaller firms that may not be able to bid for 200 km stretch, but would participate effectively and bring down the rates considerably if the stretch of road is broken into 10 to 20 parts of 10 to 20 km length each with a value of about Rs. 50 to100 crores only.

The subletting makes matters further worse as was witnessed in the case of Delhi Metro when the pillar gave way. There was no one to take responsibility as the contract of DMRC was with one party, but that party sublet the work to the other and now tried to pass on the responsibility to it. But DMRC has no agreement or official relation with it, nor can it force this firm. This of course is a legal tangle. Besides the problems in fixing responsibility, the rates also go high as more and more agencies participate in the process of outsourcing every process practically.

Hospitality Industry

This is another industry that generates and soaks huge amount of black money as sand soaks water. The sole problem with this industry is that the transactions are normally in cash whether it is a dhaba, restaurant, sweet shop, teashop, chain like Barista, chat shop or eatery of any other description including the banquets and the five star hotels. Cash transactions anywhere and everywhere lead to generation and absorption of black money. A limit of Rs. 25,000 has been imposed on cash transactions in five star hotels and beyond that cap any transaction in cash has to be accompanied by a copy each of the PAN card, the residence and the identity proof. For one, this limit is too high for day to day transactions that are repetitive in nature. Second, there are various ways to beat the cap. The bill can be split into parts each below Rs. 25,000 and the whole of the payment can be made in cash. The host alone can shell out all the cash amounting to say Rs. 2.5 lacs for the 10 bills that may be prepared in separate names for a single party. The management and the staff are too obliging and cooperative. Further, fake PAN CARDS are not at all difficult to procure and also there is no problem in giving fake address proof as well, particularly when one knows that there will be no immediate verifications. The other part of the hospitality industry connected with marriages would be dealt with in the next section. On this account there is no difference in principle in a small roadside eatery and a five star hotel except that the magnitude of transactions is very small at the former as compared to the latter. Thousands of small shops may not have any impact as a single five star hotel will have. The permissible cap for cash transaction needs be limited to Rs. 500 or at the most to Rs. 1000.

Marriage Industry

It is well known that the marriage, the jewellery and the house construction attract maximum black money in India. Indian marriage is a very elaborate affair with a series of ceremonies and corresponding celebrations, all steeped in money, mostly black. Each occasion involves entertainment and giving/taking gifts. All this involves money. Major expenses are required for jewellery, clothing, hospitality, hiring of venue, gifts and dowry. Before average expenditure on a marriage is assessed, it will be advantageous to have some idea about the number of marriages that take place during a year. The narrative proposes to study and present the analysis in context of Delhi about which the information keeps appearing in the media.

Very often we hear of traffic jams in Delhi at night because of the large number of marriages on a particular night. The number very often is quoted at 20 to 30 thousand and occasionally reaches upto 40,000. As per a news item from Gaurav Vivek Bhatnagar in the *Hindu* of 11 March 2006, there were 40,000 to 50000 marriages everyday for 20 days between the months of April and June. That puts the number between 8 and 10 lac marriages per quarter. Since marriages are not evenly distributed over the year, one cannot simply multiply it by 4 to give an annual figure, but one can be sure that the number of marriages that take place in Delhi is at least 10 lacs for the entire year. With a population of 1.8 crores as at present and over 40 lac eligibles between the age group of 20 to 29, the figure appears to be plausible. The same newspaper reverts to this issue on 13 February 2008 and states that lots of people come from outside to celebrate marriages in Delhi. Actual number may thus be much higher, but this analysis proposes to treat 10 lacs as the basic annual number of marriages in Delhi.

Some of the marriages are very simple, in jhuggi jhonparis. Though the newspaper had no reason to include these in its statistics as these do not disturb traffic or cause any ripple as these people can afford only a simple marriage in the Mohalla. But still it is proposed to leave out half of the total out of our reckoning so as to make analysis more authentic. At least 50 percent or 5 lac will be high-end marriages, of which one lac would possibly be ultra high-end. Ultra high-end marriages are celebrated in five star hotels and the super marriages take place in elaborately specially erected *Shamianas*. Expenditure on the last category is astronomical. Let us however take all these one lac under five star category. The five star hotels of private sector charge between Rs.3,000 and Rs.5,000 per plate including normal drinks (the rate for some vintage drinks could be as high as Rs. 10 lacs per bottle of a litre capacity). No doubt, it includes the rental charges for venue but extra charges are levied for decoration. However, in public sector hotels the charges are lower by almost 25 percent in comparison to private sector. Whosoever patronizes the five star hotels will have a guest list of not less than 1000. So he shells out at least Rs. 30 lacs for these two items taking basic rate of Rs. 3,000 per plate for one single occasion. In every such marriage in Delhi, there are normally five functions of which the two major functions are the marriage proper and the reception organized by the boy's side after the marriage. That function is also equally elaborate and requires similar expenses. So the expenditure on every such marriage is at least to the tune of Rs. 60 lacs or Rs. 60,000 crores for the one lac marriages on hospitality alone.

Coming to the remaining four lac marriages that are arranged through the caterers in the banquet halls, hotels other than five star or farm houses; also spend at least Rs. 2000 on an average of per plate including the cost of venue, tentage, decoration, drinks etc., the total expenditure for a moderate guest list of 800 will amount to Rs.16 lacs per function or Rs. 32 lacs for the two functions of the marriage. The total expenditure on this account for four lac marriages will amount to Rs. 12,8000 crores. When added it gives a figure of Rs. 1.88 lac crores for the Ultra high end and the high end marriages alone.

It is not possible to have any data to quantify the value of clothing and the jewellery but at the minimum, the expenditure would be no less than Rs. 50 lacs and Rs. 20 lacs respectively for the above two categories of marriages, adding Rs. 50,000 crores and Rs. 80,000 crores respectively making a total of Rs. 1,30,000 crores. So, in totality the marriage industry of Delhi alone is worth not less than a whopping sum of Rs. 3,18,000 crores.

In hotels, particularly the five star hotels, taxes are not avoidable, but when cash is accepted, the black money on which the income tax has not been paid, gets utilized. If payments were not accepted in cash, there would be a strong reason and compulsion to bring the money in the accounted stream. That covers only the expenditure of Rs. 60,000 crores whereas bulk of the remaining Rs. 2,58,000 crores income flow is in the black stream on which VAT is evaded to the extent of at least Rs. 25,800 crores taking just 10 percent for all the indirect taxes. Besides, there would be huge evasion on account of income tax. Let us take a rate of just 20 percent as against the general income tax rate of 30 percent as some of the income may be from the recorded stream, but still the evasion of income tax would be as high as Rs. 51,600 crores, raising the total tax evasion in context of marriages in Delhi alone to Rs. 77,400 crores. The implications of tax evasion and the use of black money in marriages etc at all India level can be anybody's guess.

Black Money in SEZ

SEZ is a very good concept as a hub of industrial activity and a facilitator for industrial growth. It leads to the growth of general as also the particular industrial infrastructure and also to the planned growth of the industry along with housing, market areas, educational institutions, all growing together and supporting one another. The sort of new townships that are likely to emerge will have all the modern facilities and as such can act growth bombs at the same time being the clean modern settlements as against the existing dirty old towns. But unfortunately SEZ have been drawn into serious controversies, have assumed proportion of big scams and sources of generation of black money and concentration of power. Under the garb of developing the industry, huge chunk of land is arranged to be purchased for each SEZ. These lands arranged in bulk lie unused for a number of years. A few years later only, they develop and commence sales at very high price bearing no relation with what they had paid. It has many adverse effects on the economy commencing with the bungling right at the stage of purchase of land. Sometime, part of the land is passed on to the organizers of the SEZ by the state on the pretext of public interest. The source of the land is the farmer only. When acquisition is made under the Land Acquisition Act in public interest, the compensation is rather on lower side. Basically, the private promoter acquires this part of the land at throw away prices as the price charged by the state from him is directly in accordance with what the state had paid at the time of acquisition. It will be another story that the promoter might have to bribe the concerned authorities as came out in the media in context of the big corporate Satyam scam. Some of the land is acquired afresh also. All acquisition by the state is at low prices and have the effect of transfer of economic power to the developer of the SEZ. Further once the intention of the state to acquire a chunk of land in a particular area gets known and the process of acquisition commences, panic spreads that the land will be acquired at rock bottom low rates. Even the neighbouring farmers then sell their lands to the organizers of the SEZ at prices just marginally higher than the acquisition rates. It was seen in Gurgaon that once such panic spread, the farmers made a beeline to sell their land to the organizer of the SEZ to mop up whatever excess they could, over the rates offered by the state. Action of the state in acquiring part of the land and creating panic thus has an effect of compelling the farmers to sell lands at low rates in order to escape still lower rates under acquisition. Once the panic ridden farmers sell the land to the SEZ, it is widely advertised both by the government and the SEZ management that the farmers have willingly sold their lands. A completely false statement, but the poor simple farmers remain helpless and cannot do anything.

As mentioned earlier once the land has been purchased/ acquired, it is allowed to lie undeveloped for a few years. By then the authorized institutional /market /industrial space gets exhausted and the prices for any land or building in these areas skyrocket. People establish business/industry in unauthorized areas. They are then threatened by the authorities with eviction and other penal consequences for violation of laws. They cough up money in bribes to get the same regularized and at this stage are also ready to pay much higher prices for regular plots / buildings. At that time the organizers of SEZ throw open a part of their estate slowly in bits raising the price every now and then. Some of the builders in Gurgaon are still disposing of buildings on land acquired in 80s or 90s. They had purchased this land at very low prices say in thousands or in a few lacs per acre. Now it takes that amount to purchase just one square yard from the colonizers/ builders.

The ill-effects are manifold. First of all, the economic development slows down as a number of entrepreneurs who would have started business/industry if only they could get land at affordable rates, are dissuaded from putting up their ventures. Not only they are deprived of their legitimate business, but that also leads to lower employment and less of growth of the economy that otherwise would have taken place, defeating thereby the very rationale of creation of the SEZ. Second, it leads to higher costs as the entrepreneur would violate law at every stage and for that has to grease the palm of some state functionary or the other. Third, the lands lie fallow for long times, leading to direct loss of production. Fourth, since the land is sold at a later stage at very high rates, the sale invariably involves a huge black content. Even the corporate developers are no exception. Some four years ago, I approached one of the big corporate builders for office accommodation. Ostensibly, he was conducting transactions in white money, but when it came to the question of actual payment, the corporate builder wanted only Rs.1800 per sft by cheque and remaining Rs. 2700 per sft in cash i.e. in black. Obviously I did not purchase and the transaction was dropped, but it shows that even the corporate developers are no exception to black transactions. All have evolved different ways and means for the black economy and black transactions. Fifth, the undue concentration of power develops in a few hands. Once non-extendable natural resource like land is so occupied, the society can be held to ransom by the developer. The live example is that of Ambani brothers who are holding the country to ransom in case of gas from KG basin. The gas could have flowed into use four years back, may be for generation of electricity, for running railways, for running vehicles or as cooking gas, the nation would have gained and that would also have saved the foreign exchange. Besides, perhaps more important, employment could have been generated for thousands/lacs of unemployed youth, but all that has been lost. Nation is not interested in whether the fight of the brothers is real or as observed by the CJI, a stage managed drama where they want to delay and charge higher rates. Even if it is a genuine corporate fight, it is basically the fight between the two dons, over share in the distribution of spoils at the cost of the country that has been denied the use of its own natural wealth. The country has been deprived of the growth for full four years and caused strain on other crucial resources. May be that jungles would have been saved if the gas was available as fuel or the fertilizers produced by this gas would have meant ample supplies at reduced rates to the farmer that would have given a fillip to agricultural production warding off the present scarcity. Lastly, there is another aspect too. The Land Ceiling Act does not permit concentration of land in any single individual in agriculture sector. There is a well considered rationale to it that land is a limited resource and cannot be created, so nobody should own more than his immediate needs. Since the industry requires more land than a farming unit, so the relaxation in favour of industry is logical. But at the same time the land cannot be allowed to lie fallow, create scarcities and make speculative gains for the organizers of the SEZ. In the present form, the SEZs are the great explosive device that will concentrate economic power and impart a capacity to exploit. That, in the long run, will push costs upwards and slow the very economic growth that it was supposed to accelerate, thereby pushing the nation on to a destructive path.

As mentioned earlier there are important positive aspects of SEZ as an industrial development device that is a key to solution of unemployment problem and for the rapid planned and systematic growth of the nation. Frightening the industry from Singur was a very disastrous step by Mamta Banerjee, but unfortunately, the politics in our country can be quite destructive as national interest does not find any place in the calculations of the political parties, whatever be their shade. Now, however, what Mamta Baneerjee is saying about the SEZ makes sense. Her latest stance is that she is not against SEZ provided the land is purchased in the open market and secondly it is developed, offered and sold to industry within five years of purchase otherwise the land should lapse to the government. It appears to be a very sensible suggestion as the use of land for purposes of empire building would stop. I would go a step further to the extent that if the land is not finally developed and disposed in five years from the date of acquiring/purchasing, it should not only lapse to the state but the organizer should not be paid any compensation for purchasing it or for developing it. That will check the speculative and the empire building tendencies that the real estate sector has been pursuing. More important from our point of view is that the step will reduce the generation and use of black money and the resultant evasion of taxes.

Black Delhi

It would be interesting to see the macro situation in totality on territorial basis for one state and no state would be better suited for the purpose than Delhi that we have also analysed partially at micro-level. As outlined above, the real figures can never come out whatever be the survey or the analysis. Figures apart, even the existing real situation is not allowed to surface normally. It was due to certain extraordinary events in the capital that threw open these secrets. In 2001, the Supreme Court ruled to move the polluting and dangerous industries out of Delhi. Instantaneously the huge numbers of industries and the industrial workers that never existed on record so far sprang up. These numbers were manifold in comparison to the declared official statistics so far. The stunning accounts came out in context of obtaining concessions from the court as also from the state. The new revelations placed the number of total industrial units at 140000 as against the authorized number of only 22000 units that is 118000 were reported functioning in the unrecorded sector in which, among other things, evasion of taxes and generation of black money was a rule.

Delhi may be starved of water, but is floating on the ocean of black money. A perceptive eye can see money itself floating around in the air in the polluted Delhi environment and this fact is borne out time and again whenever it becomes necessary to bring the real picture before the public. It had become unavoidable in the wake of relocation of industries in the year 2001 when the startling figures of 22-40 lacs (varying between different sources) of workers employed by polluting/unauthorized industries in Delhi came out. It was compulsion not only on the part of the industry, but also the politician who hunted for votes by taking this side or that. Many other denominations had varied interests in placing the grave situation before the court, the government and the people for gaining sympathy as the large number of workers who were going to be affected as part of the relocation of the industries in the city of Delhi posed a serious human problem. Not the entire industry of Delhi was being relocated but only those units that were in unauthorized areas and were also a source of pollution. But the number of such industrial units came out to no less than 1,18,000 with huge number of people working with them.

In 2006 again Delhi was on trial on the issue of unauthorized shops and commercial units in the residential areas. The magnitude came to notice as the number of shops in the unauthorized areas posed a real big problem and the issue of their relocation was taken up by the High Court and the Supreme Court. It was astonishing that as high a number as 35 lac workers were employed by these shops that had to be closed down. It naturally turned into a big human problem as they all would lose their jobs. Nobody earlier thought that Delhi provided employment to such a large number. But this vast number of employees is unaccounted and unrecorded, so the value addition by them remains in black economy and also their compensation comes from shady area though they also put in their sweat and blood. The workers earn their wages, but the employers corner the surplus that remains unaccounted.

If for industry, we take the median figure at 30 lac workers that were to be relocated as a result of the relocation of the factories and 35 lac for the shops that were to be shifted as per the account of the reputed journalist Prem Shankar Jha in the *Outlook* of 10 April 2006; there were a total of 65 lac unaccounted workers in these two sectors alone. Presuming that these industrial/shop workers were drawing on an average emoluments of just Rs. 50,000 per annum at that time, their total compensation will amount to Rs. 32,500 crores per year.

Then there must be at least half the number of workes who are borne on the records of the industries and shops that are functioning in lawful premises, the total wage bill in Delhi state adds upto Rs. 49000 crores.

The number of employees in the PSUs, the local bodies, Delhi state government and the Central government employees located in Delhi was 7.81 lacs at that very time. They include a large number of highly paid officers and staff, but taking the average annual salary just @ 2.0 lacs PA only, their pay bill will also add to Rs.15620 crores. Thus in Delhi, the total wage bill by itself will add upto Rs. 64620 crores as against the total official GDP figures of Rs. 77185 crores for the year, whereas we have yet to account for the high income strata of the society as we have not included the income of the corporate sector, the industrialist, the shop-ownesr, the professionals like architects, doctors, advocates, engineers ,consultants ,chartered accountants, contractors and also have not touched certain sectors like transport and its ancillaries like petrol pumps, the repair garages and many more including the big construction industry as a whole, that the state of Delhi boasts of.

These are all high category income groups. If an amount of Rs. 64620 crores accrues as wages/salaries earned in Delhi, all these high end categories recounted above and the unsaid denominations may be earning at least double the amount including their black earnings, the total real GDP of Delhi would be at least of the order of Rs. 193860 crores in place of mere Rs. 77185 crores .

This gives unaccounted income stream of Rs. 1.165 lacs crores for the limited segment of the economy. The income earned by labour may not attract provisions of income tax but the income earned by all other categories is subject to the personal taxation. Excepting Rs. 32500 crores earned as wages in unaccounted sector, all the remaining income of Rs. 84,000 crores out of Rs. 1.165 lac crores is subject to income tax. At 30 percent, the additional income tax collected from Delhi should not be less than Rs. 25200 crores. Besides income tax the collection of sales tax will get a big boost. Once wages are paid off the record, the whole production automatically will be unrecorded and so will be the sales. Since sales tax is on the sale of goods, we have to estimate figures of production against a wage bill of Rs. 49000 crores. If it is just tenfold i.e. the ratio between the wages and the sale price of the commodities produced is 1:10, the total production in Delhi should be something like Rs. 490000 crores. Even if sales tax is calculated only @ 5 percent of the total production, the tax will amount to Rs. 24500 crores as against Rs. 5000 crores collected in 2006-07 excluding the tax on petrol.

These are astronomical figures that one finds difficult to digest. To test check I decided to visit various markets to get first hand feel of the ground situation. I visited Sadar Bazaar, the timber market, the building material market, the cloth market and the catering industry. I spent quite some time in observing and then talking to the shopkeepers, sympathizing with them for their compulsions to indulge in all this. When they opened up, they all confessed that their recorded business by and large averaged to only 10 percent or so of the real magnitude. The percentage may be higher with corporate world, but surely the overall collection will not project beyond 15 percent. Whatever discount may be given still the hidden economy and the evasion of taxes consequentially is just mind boggling.

Delhi is a very big center of trade, commerce and industry, where production from areas not only around, but from far and wide comes to the wholesale market for distribution and taxes become due on those sales as also on the incomes accruing thereby. The position of Delhi may be worse, but position everywhere in the country is bad enough. All the metropolises will more or less follow the model of Delhi.

Delhi is a very big market but tax collections from sales tax/VAT etc. amount only to peanut as Delhi collected Rs. 8310 crores only, during 2007-08. A significant proportion of sales tax in Delhi comes from sale of petroleum products, for which latest figures could not be available, but the statistics for the earlier years put this ratio at about 40 percent, the same can be adopted for 2007-08 as no relative changes occur in the short run. If at all any change is visualized, the tax revenue on oil should have jumped in view of the high oil prices. At this rate in 2007-08, out of a total amount of Rs. 8310 collected in sales tax, the contribution of all other commodities would amount to Rs. 4986 crores only.

The above are some of the practical illustrations of how the slush is generated. In our country no reason, rationale or long drawn process is required to generate black money. It is literally generated out of the thin air. I personally encountered a very interesting but a shocking situation in 1995 when I came across an instance of how our resources were being drained away and how costs of production were being pushed up, making ours a black money generating, high-cost economy uncompetitive in world markets. I propose to share the same.

At a social gathering, on my being ushered into the party, a person working as General Manager of a urea plant was introduced to me, but the host missed introducing me to him. The man appeared to be on his second or third large drink and was absolutely frank and truthful. I learnt from him that his firm had three-four units producing fertilizers. Urea was in news those days and the scandals in its import were being talked about. It was only a year later that the great Urea scandal became public. The scandal was unique in the sense that the entire amount was paid in advance and whole of it had disappeared without delivering a grain of fertilizer, as against certain percentage as kickbacks in other cases.

I inquired why our industry was so irresponsible that it produced urea at double the global prices. The gentleman confided in me that the roots of the high costs lay deep in the industrial houses and the government. He narrated that a few years back, he was asked to prepare a scheme for a new plant designed for a particular capacity. He prepared a proposal for Rs. 350 crores. The management asked him to raise it to Rs. 700 crore in a way that Rs. 300 crores could be kept aside abroad, of which Rs. 100 crores would go to the authorities in the Central Government as hush money and the remaining will constitute deposits abroad for the industrial house itself. The balance of Rs. 50 crore would create the necessary cushion for use within the country i.e. it would be black money within. The people in government would not agree for less than Rs. 200 crore, which the industrial enterprise was not prepared to part with, so the deal fell.

The stalemate continued for a few years before the exercise was resumed. In the meantime, the fair estimate worked out to Rs. 700 crore. This time the industrialist had a prior discussion and the share of those in government was pegged in advance at Rs. 400 crore. The house planned its own deposits abroad amounting to Rs. 400 crore and kept another Rs. 100 crores aside for any exigency and hiked the project cost to Rs. 1600 crores. If fixed costs are hiked from Rs. 350 to 700 crores and Rs. 700 to 1600 crores, the costs of production have to go up. He blamed the corruption in the Government for all this with contemptuous reference to politicians as *KUTTAS (the greedy dogs)* and the civil servants as *PILLAS (the greedy puppies)*. When I asked him how about his masters, he was very candid that if only people in government were clean, they only would have prevented his masters. Very proudly he declared that their old plant that had come up in the good old days was producing urea at the rate of Rs. 3000 per ton as against Rs. 8000 per ton of this new plant. There was a subsidy of Rs. 4000 per ton and they sold their entire produce at Rs. 4000 per ton in the market and that his factory was making huge profits. In any case, the industrial house had recovered its entire investment by withdrawal of its own funds even before the factory commenced its operations.

The above narrations and incidents give an idea how the black money is being generated, tossed around and created out of nothing. Even small industries carry within them huge underbelly of reserves in black. Actually, the ways of the black economy are curious and inscrutable. Its penetration is too deep, its coverage too wide and its extent too large. Then it not only operates inland but is closely knit with operations and the banking channels abroad. God alone knows how much out of it is taken abroad, how much is invested locally and how much is stacked in cash. Such issues and the magnitude of the problem are examined in the ensuing chapters.

3

Tax Evasion and Magnitude of Black Money

In India, ever since the Independence our business and industry have been at great pains to drive home that tax rates in our country have been very high and that has always been cited as a justification for evasion of taxes. There is no doubt that the tax rates in India at one stage were very high with the rate of income tax peaking at 97.7 percent in the year 1973-74. On the other hand the collection of union taxes continued to be one of the lowest in the world at 4.32 percent of the GDP in 1950-51, of which direct taxes formed only 1.88 percent. With the rising rates, the amount of taxes collected did go up, but only slightly and remained on a single digit till the year 2003-04. Even in 1973-74 when the marginal rate of individual tax was as high as 97.7 percent and so were the rates of indirect taxes, the total collection was only 8.18 percent of which direct taxes constituted only 2.22 percent of the GDP. For the first time in 2003-04 the amount collected as taxes by the Union Government crossed into the double digits and is 10 plus at present as against the world average of 26 percent for the central taxes. The situation in states is no better. Even when all the state taxes all over the country are included, the ratio of total taxes collected to GDP works out to 17.7 percent in 2008 as against 36 percent in OECD countries and many other countries all over the world. If our tax rates are higher than other countries, why our tax collections fall short in comparison to them as percentage of the GDP. With higher rates, our collections should also be higher, but evasion being general, our collections fall short. Figures of Tax to GDP ratio for the OECD countries are given in Table 3.1 and the same for 179 countries the world over is attached as annexure "D". Our position in the world is also fairly bad. Even in the third world most of the countries are better than us. (See Table 3.1)

As usual excuses are cited for our dismal performance in this field as well and in this case the most touted reason is that we are a poor country and economically lower denominations of the society are too poor to be subjected to any taxation. The argument holds no water as all the sections are subject to the indirect taxes at the same uniform rate. Secondly, we are not talking of the absolute or the total collections but percentages only. So far as share of various denominations in National cake is concerned, India is far better placed than the US even as per the World Bank's World Development Report 1999-2000. The share of lowest 10 percent of population in India was 4.1 percent and in the USA the same was at 1.5 percent only. For next 10 percent of population the figures for India and the USA were 5.1 and 3.3 percent respectively. It is a different matter that our unaccounted sector has not been included otherwise we may steeply go down, but then all the calculations are on our declared incomes and so are we looking for taxes here. The relative capacity of an Indian on an average should be higher than that of an American, but since in recorded economy also there is steep tax evasion by the higher echelons of society, that explains the lower percentage of tax collections in India.

Table 3.1: Total tax revenue as percentage of GDP

	1975	1985	1990	1995	2000	2004	2005	2006	2007 Provisional
Canada	32.0	32.5	35.9	35.6	35.6	33.7	33.4	33.3	33.3
Mexico	17.0	17.3	16.7	18.5	19.0	19.9	20.6	20.5	
United States	25.6	25.6	27.3	27.9	29.9	26.1	27.3	28.0	28.3
Australia	25.8	28.3	28.5	28.8	31.1	31.1	30.8	30.6	n.a
Japan	20.9	27.4	29.1	26.8	27.0	26.3	27.4	27.9	n.a
Korea	15.1	16.4	18.9	19.4	23.6	24.6	25.5	26.8	28.7
New Zealand	28.5	31.1	37.4	36.6	33.6	35.3	37.5	36.7	36.0
Austria	36.7	40.9	39.6	41.2	42.6	42.8	42.1	41.7	41.9
Belgium	39.5	44.4	42.0	43.6	44.9	44.8	44.8	44.5	44.4
Czech Republic	37.5	35.3	37.8	37.5	36.9	36.4			
Denmark	38.4	46.1	46.5	48.8	49.4	49.0	50.7	49.1	48.9
Finland	36.5	39.7	43.5	45.7	47.2	43.4	43.9	43.5	43.0
France	35.4	42.8	42.0	42.9	44.4	43.5	43.9	44.2	43.6
Germany	34.3	36.1	34.8	37.2	37.2	34.8	34.8	35.6	36.2
Greece	19.4	25.5	26.2	28.9	34.1	31.2	31.3	31.3	n.a.
Hungary	41.3	38.0	37.6	37.2	37.1	39.3			
Iceland	30.0	28.2	30.9	31.2	37.2	38.0	40.7	41.5	41.4
Ireland	28.7	34.6	33.1	32.5	31.7	30.1	30.6	31.9	32.2

Contd...

Italy	25.4	33.6	37.8	40.1	42.3	41.0	40.9	42.1	43.3
Luxembourg	32.8	39.5	35.7	37.1	39.1	37.3	37.8	35.9	36.9
Netherlands	40.7	42.4	42.9	41.5	39.7	37.3	38.8	39.3	38.0
Norway	39.2	42.6	41.0	40.9	42.6	43.3	43.5	43.9	43.4
Poland	36.2	31.6	32.3	32.9	33.5	n.a			
Portugal	19.7	25.2	27.7	31.7	34.1	33.9	34.7	35.7	36.6
Slovak Republic	33.8	31.8	31.8	29.8	29.8				
Spain	18.4	27.6	32.5	32.1	34.2	34.6	35.8	36.6	37.2
Sweden	41.2	47.3	52.2	47.5	51.8	48.7	49.5	49.1	48.2
Switzerland	23.9	25.5	25.8	27.7	30.0	28.8	29.2	29.6	29.7
Turkey	11.9	11.5	14.9	16.8	24.2	24.1	24.3	24.5	23.7
United Kingdom	35.2	37.6	36.1	34.5	37.1	35.4	36.3	37.1	36.6
Unweighted average:									
OECD Total	29.4	32.7	33.8	34.8	36.1	35.2	35.8	35.9	n.a
OECD America	28.8	25.0	26.8	26.7	28.0	26.2	26.9	27.3	27.4
OECD Pacific	22.6	25.8	28.5	27.9	28.8	29.3	30.3	30.5	n.a
OECD Europe	30.9	35.3	36.1	37.1	38.4	37.5	38.0	38.0	n.a
EU 19	32.2	37.6	38.2	38.9	39.4	38.3	38.7	38.7	n.a
EU 15	32.2	37.6	38.2	39.0	40.6	39.2	39.7	39.8	n.a
n.a indicates not available.									
India	12.59	15.48	17.01	14.64	14.98	16.31	17.17	18.17	18.44

It is often said that the high rates of personal income tax in free India led to evasion of taxes and creation of black money. If the rates were so high, why the collection of direct taxes was only 1.88 percent of the GDP in 1950-51. Basic problem is that evasion was rampant at that time also and that led to setting up of Vardachari Commission on tackling tax evasion. It was on the report of this Commission that the first Voluntary Disclosure Scheme was introduced in 1951, but like all its successors it met with failure. The only purpose it served was that some of the people were able to convert their black money into white at no cost or at best at low cost. At that time there used to be the concept of Super Income slab. Rates of tax that are hyped were high only for this bracket which was applicable to very high income levels, but not in general as the people from business and industry like to believe. As late as 1952-53, the rate of personal tax on an income of Rs. 24000 was 12 percent after adjusting the exemption limit. The rate of corporation tax was 12.5 percent till 1949-50, raised to 15.5 percent in 1950-51 and to 17 percent in 1951-52. Even at that low rate of corporation tax, the collection of direct taxes did not touch even the meager 2 percent till the Chinese aggression in 1962-63. The budget speeches of the then Finance Ministers show that they were not finding the compliance to improve. They were constantly trying manipulating one tax or the other, but with no success. In the process they experimented with raising/lowering as also abolishing and introducing various taxes, but failed. It appears the patriotic fervour in the wake of Chinese aggression lasted till 1965-66, as the collections again fell to 1.89 in 1967-68, touching almost the level of 1950-51. This sordid performance led to raising the rate of taxation that peaked at 97 percent for personal tax in 1973-74. Tax rates had to be raised because of low compliance and not that the high rates were the cause of low compliance as is generally made out to be.

During emergency, because of fear of action, the compliance again rose from 2.25 in 1974-75 to 2.80 in 1975-76 and maintained the level till 1976-77. After the emergency, the enforcement slackened and so did the collections that again slumped to 2.50 in 1977-78 and continued that way till 1990-91 touching a low of 2.06 percent. This shows that the tax collection is more elastic to the action of the enforcement agencies rather than anything else. However, it must be made clear that at the same time the tax rates have to be realistic.

In any case with steep reduction in all the tax rates in recent past, India falls under average tax rate regimes in the world, so the basic objection of trade, commerce and industry has been met with, but we still continue to be very high on the ladder of evasion and clamour of the lobbies to lower the tax rates further continues. But they are also opposed to Kelkar model that lowers the tax rates, but eliminates all the exemptions and levies personal tax on gross incomes as that would greatly reduce evasion on recorded incomes at least. In the world wherever tax rates are lower, similar models have been adopted. In that model manipulations on accounted incomes are by and large ruled out. What all these statistics tell is, *prima facie* the story of the recoded income alone. When unrecorded incomes are also clubbed together, the real percentage of tax to GDP may decline steeply to something like 7 to 8 from the 17.7 percent as the official statistics reveal. There is bigger evasion of taxes on unrecorded GDP as that is subject to tax in full for two reasons that mostly the unrecorded GDP belongs to higher sections of society whose income is subject to higher slabs of taxation and secondly they have already availed of all the exemptions, rebates and discounts.

There have been quite a few attempts from time to time and various estimates have been advanced placing black economy at 20 percent in fifties to 50 percent in seventies through the eighties. Now it is believed that 50 percent of the GDP is accounted and the other 50 percent remains in the unrecorded sector or there is an equal parallel economy running as compared to the official economy. *Prima facie* it may appear to be an exaggeration, but is not so when analysed thoroughly from many angles with an open mind.

It may be recalled that the few industries (some of them being insignificant) that have been examined in the preceding chapter, have thrown up formidable statistics related to tax evasion and creation of black money. Viewed together in Table 3.2 below, it presents a very sordid dismal story.

Table 3.2: Tax evasion and black money creation

(In crores of rupees)

Name of Industry	Taxes evaded	Black economy generated
Beedi (all India)	6000	18257
Gold Jewellery (India)	75000	500000
Trucking industry (all India)	126000	377964
Admission to Medical Colleges (all India)	--	20000
Construction industry	50000	Not estimable
Marriage industry (Delhi)	77400	258000
Card Printing (Delhi)	1890	15750
Hospitality ....Not estimable..........................		
SEZ ....do.................................		
Builder...............................do.................................		
Property Registry ....do.................................		
Infrastructure ....do.................................		
Delhi State	49700	116500

The above are only by way of example or the sample that a few aspects have been taken into account. Story in each and every sector is similar. Once one evades one tax, and the incomes are brought to the black sector, many more taxes are evaded. There are many industries in which quantifying is not possible as can be inferred from the details attempted in the earlier chapter.

Hospitality, infrastructure, registry and many more, some of which have been analysed in the previous chapter, fall in that category.

Taking view of a state in totality, Delhi alone as per our peripheral analysis, accounts for generation of a black component of 1.165 lac crores and evasion of taxes to the extent of Rs. 49,700 crores. Both the Union and the Delhi governments need to wake up from their slumber.

Such huge evasion is possible as the elite consider misappropriation of taxes as a perk and a privilege as pointed by Gorwala as early as in 1951. The Committee examined the macro aspects from the angle of evasion of taxes. As quoted in the introduction, he brought out clearly how the big people were evading taxes while small men were even unnecessarily being harassed. The same holds good to this day and evasion of taxes with all the other consequential aberrations continue unabated. Gorwala was rightly worried and was very correct as despite the much hyped high rates of taxes, the total collection as taxes by the Centre and the states was as low as 6.69 percent of the GDP in 1950-51 and made very tardy progress subsequently. Against the average of about 30 percent in the advanced economies of the world at that time and collection of taxes reaching 35 to 40 percent of the GDP (as per Table 3.1) for the well meaning OECD countries and annexure "D" for other countries, whereas in India after the much talked recent hikes, the rate is still a poor 17.7 percent of the GDP for both Centre and states combined. This is for the arithmetic of the accounted portion of the economy. There is parallel unaccounted economy. Though accounts of Delhi put the unrecorded economy many times the recorded one, the total size of the economy can be taken at least double of what is recorded. As mantioned above when the unaccounted parallel economy is added, the rate of collection of taxes will fall to a dismal 7 percent of the GDP. Vast amounts that should have gone to the exchequer have been and are being misappropriated as is clear from Table 3.3.

The Table gives figures of the GDP and the amount of taxes collected by the Union Government and all the state governments. It proceeds to indicate what percentage of GDP should have been collected and what has actually been collected and finally how much has been the evasion. All these figures are in terms of the percentages of GDP and in the last column the actual amount of evasion has been worked out into the absolute numbers.

Table 3.3: Computation of Tax Evaded

Year	GDP at Current prices	GDP 93-94 Constant prices	State & Central Taxes Realized percentage of GDP	Percentage of GDP due as Taxes	Taxes evaded as percentage of GDP	Amount of Tax evaded
1950-51	9678	140466	6.69	25	18.31	25719
1951-52	10227	143745	7.42	25	17.58	25270
1952-53	10095	147824	6.94	25	18.06	26697
1953-54	11000	156822	6.32	25	18.68	29294
1954-55	10322	163479	7.15	25	17.85	29181
1955-56	10508	167667	7.49	25	17.51	29358
1956-57	12539	177211	7.28	25	17.72	31402
1957-58	12817	175068	8.29	25	16.71	29254
1958-59	14325	188354	7.76	25	17.26	32510
1959-60	15026	192476	8.22	25	16.78	32297
1960-61	16440	206103	8.33	25	16.67	34357
1961-62	17326	212499	8.98	25	16.02	34042
1962-63	18523	216994	10.09	25	14.91	32354
1963-64	21181	227980	10.95	25	14.05	32031
1964-65	24731	245270	10.58	25	14.42	35368
1965-66	25883	236306	11.18	25	13.82	32657
1966-67	29417	238710	11.03	25	13.97	33348

Contd...

1967-68	34582	258137	9.99	25	15.01	38746
1968-69	36486	264873	10.25	25	14.75	39069
1969-70	40134	282134	10.4	25	14.6	41191
1970-71	42697	296278	11.01	25	13.99	41450
1971-72	45440	299269	12.05	30	17.95	53718
1972-73	50002	298316	12.62	30	17.38	51847
1973-74	61324	311894	11.92	30	18.08	56390
1974-75	72275	315514	12.59	30	17.41	54931
1975-76	76816	343924	14.2	30	15.8	54340
1976-77	82612	348223	14.53	30	15.47	53870
1977-78	94319	374235	13.78	30	16.22	60700
1978-79	101463	394828	14.9	30	15.1	59619
1979-80	111040	374291	15.46	30	14.04	52550
1980-81	132865	401128	14.59	30	15.41	61814
1981-82	155198	425073	15.11	30	14.89	63293
1982-83	172703	438079	15.29	30	14.71	64441
1983-84	201806	471742	15.19	30	14.81	69865
1984-85	226270	492077	15.48	30	14.42	70957
1985-86	252998	513990	16.5	30	13.5	69389
1986-87	281876	536257	16.91	30	13.09	70196
1987-88	318970	556778	17.1	30	12.9	71824
1988-89	379294	615098	16.91	30	12.09	74365
1989-90	436403	656331	17.01	30	12.99	85257
1990-91	507487	692871	16.38	30	13.62	94369
1991-92	584091	701863	16.73	30	13.27	93137
1992-93	669872	737792	16.17	30	13.83	102037
1993-94	781345	781345	14.19	30	15.81	123531
TOTAL		**15419318**				**2298043**
Converted to 2008=09 price Level		**38394101.8**				**5722127**

Contd...

At 2008-09 prices						
1994-95	912156	1877081	14.64	35	20.36	382173
1995-96	1069805	2131051	14.83	35	20.17	429833
1996-97	1247628	2284260	14.76	35	20.24	462334
1997-98	1388729	2435165	14.06	35	20.94	509923
1998-99	1601114	2605734	13.76	35	21.24	553458
1999-2000	1771094	2773600	14.98	35	20.02	555274
2000-01	1902284	2923881	16.05	35	18.95	554075
2001-02	2077658	3079386	15.1	35	19.99	615569
2002-03	2244725	3112115	16.71	35	18.29	569205
2003-04	2754620	3789504	16.31	35	18.69	708258
2004-05	3149407	4285258	17.17	35	17.83	764061
2005-06	3586743	4627455	18.17	35	16.83	778800
2006-07	4129173	4760019	18.44	35	16.56	788263
2007-08	4723400	4962559	17.7	35	17.3	858522
2008-09	5321753	5321753	17.7	35	17.3	920663
						15172598

In the above Table all the figures upto 1993-94 have been converted to the common denominator of 1993-94 prices at 100 as the base and subsequently all the figures have been further converted to current price level of 2008-09 taking the indices as per the Economic Survey 2008-09. The picture of total tax evasion over the years at 2008-09 prices is just frightening. Since 1950-51 till the present day, the amount of evasion works out to over Rs. 150 lac crores ($ 3.3 trillion) – a huge evasion. This by itself does not tell the complete story as this is the evasion on the recorded income alone. If the Tax GDP ratio all over the world is 35 percent or so, why it should not be at that level in India? Our story is further compounded by the unaccounted sector. In case of the unrecorded incomes, the whole spectrum of taxes, including the direct and the indirect, is evaded.

So the percentage of evasion on the unaccounted income would be 35 or at double the rate as on recorded incomes. As per Table 3.3, the evasion on recorded income in the year 2008-09 @ 17.3 percent works out to Rs. 9.2 lac crore. On unrecorded equal income it would amount to 18.40 lac crores or a total evasion of Rs. 27.6 lac crores for the year.

On the same analogy the total amount by way of evasion during the period 1950-51 to 2008-09, will also mount to Rs. 450 lac crores ($10 trillion) i.e. threefold the amount of Rs. 150 lac crores ($3.3 trillion) on 2008-09 prices; against which India's external debt at Rs. 10 lac crores ($ 224 bn), both for public as also private sectors, appears to be peanut.

Had the taxes been collected in a fair manner, the Indian states would have had resources for everything. We would not have been begging from one and all. Now we dole out a lot on imports and technology, the experts say that the reason is simple that we do not invest on research. Any research requires heavy investment and the return starts after a long gestation period. Private sector is naturally reluctant to go into such ventures and state does not have enough resources because of the tax evasion. So country pays in many ways, very heavily through the nose.

Not only the research, even the routine development in all the sectors and particularly in primary sector gets tardy. Let us take agriculture. A single reason cited from many angles is that the requisite capital investment has always eluded this industry. Here again corruption is responsible in two ways. First, direct for non-payment of due taxes, as explained above it is common to all the sectors and second because of the lack of education and such other factors in rural India, even that meager amount earmarked for being invested does not reach as per the oft quoted statement of Rajiv Gandhi, the then Prime Minister that only 15 paise reach the intended person in the rural sector out of every rupee the state spends for him. Now it is believed, as opined by Rahul Gandhi (who has inside access to government policies and records), during his tour of Madhya Pradesh that the actual share filtering down has declined to just 10 paise i. e. only 10 percent of the investment in rural areas is gainful and the rest literally goes down the drain. This is not the story of one state only, but of all and since the politicians of all the hues mention it with a gleeful chuckle and with force (as if it is a great achievement on their part), there is no reason to disbelieve.

At present, the annual public sector investment in rural India is placed at Rs. 1.4 lac crores. Working that out in concrete terms, it means only Rs. 14000 crores reach the intended segment though the entire amount is drawn from the exchequer. Obviously, the balance amount of Rs. 1.26 lac crores is misappropriated. Where does this huge amount disappear and who corners or misappropriates the same, is very important to investigate to pinpoint the delinquents, but that is a separate question. For our present analysis, the relevant fact is that wherever or to whoever the money may go, it converts into the unaccounted stream and forms part of the black income, of say either the civil servant, or the politician, or the contractor or any other denomination. Further, all the transactions made with it will go on multiplying through the multiplier effect as black transactions.

Last year, Yashwant Sinha, the former Union finance minister in a TV programme about Jharkhand had adduced the information from a village Sarpanch from that state that the labour in rural areas was being paid at 40 to 50 per cent of the minimum prescribed wage. Bills, of course, are prepared for full amount and the rest unpaid makes way into the black money stream of someone or the other. This, by itself generates huge chunk of black money. All this and others, when combined, constitute a mind boggling reserve of black money. May be Madhu Koda partly carried this money.

Let us look at and assess this phenomenon from another angle. Pavan Varma, a prolific writer, in his book titled *The Great Indian Middle Class*, has quoted the CII surveys of 1996 in context of assessing the projections of aggregate demands in the economy for assessment of its size in order to plan their market strategies and the sales operations. The survey "concluded that there are 180 million people in India with an annual income exceeding $3197 ....." I elaborated this point in my book *Who Owns CBI: The Naked Truth*. $ 3197 converts into Rs. 1,20,000. By itself the total income of these 18 crore people alone will add upto Rs. 21.60 lac crores annually as against our ostensible GDP figures of Rs. 13.55 lac crores that year for the entire population of the country.

Following the classification as per the World Bank, the share of the highest 20 percent in national cake is 46.1 percent and of the remaining 80 is 53.9 percent. (NSS surveys widely differ with these ratios and place the share of highest 20 percent at much higher level. That issue will be taken up in details in the subsequent chapter.) Applying the same proportion as worked out by the World Bank, the remaining population has at least an income of Rs. 25.25 lac crores, adding up to a total of Rs. 46.85 lac crores.

Thus, as per this assessment based on the CII surveys, the GNP of India at Rs.46.85 lac crores exceeds the official figure of Rs.13.55 lac crores for 1996-97 by 33.30 lac crores. In other words the unrecorded income is 2.48 times of the recorded income. The results are just startling and the extent of black money is beyond the wildest imagination.

4

The Traitor Elite

Gandhiji beautifully depicted an eternal truth concerning human nature "....there can never be enough to meet even a single individual`s greed" and India witnessed a mushrooming growth of greedy politicians, bureaucrats, businessmen (including industrialists) and professionals in the post independence era. Non –payment of taxes, misappropriation of public funds and creation of black money by them became rampant. They amassed huge reserves of black money in India and abroad. Since they were the powerful and the influential elite of the society, they could hold the laws at bay with contempt and violate them at will with impunity. All this was pointed out and placed on record formally by at least two committees namely AD Gorwala Committee on Administrative Reforms in 1951 and the Santhanam Committee on Corruption in 1964.The powerful influential people could ensure that so far as they were concerned the reports remained inoperative.

As awareness grew because of the spread of education, the media coverage and the exposition by the media, they coined and advocated justification for all their wrongs including illegal acquisitions and amassing of wealth and sought protection behind the shield of compulsions that they encountered while running the governance of the country. Basically they treat all this as perks and claim the privilege of not being proceeded against and advocate that the operation of normal laws should not apply to them as otherwise they will not be able to function effectively in the service of the country. They would like the people to believe that even all their criminal acts are in the public interest. It is as a result of the combination of these perks and privileges that the parallel black economy is flourishing and enormous sums of Indian money are lying in secret bank accounts and in the assets abroad. Recently it came under focus, but nothing much is likely to happen as every group manages to manipulate the laws and their enforcement to exclude itself.

The politician has created his right on and a justification for black money. According to him, he requires huge sums for fighting costly elections that his meagre compensation from the state does not permit. He has to live and bring up his family at certain standard and also save for the lean season when he is out of power. Nobody can grudge that he should get enough for a decent living, but where is the need for all this cobweb of bungling, black money and corruption that he has created and continues to justify? Is he not himself responsible for all this? There are ways and means to tackle all the genuine problems and the country can certainly afford to compensate him adequately in proportion to our resources and the prevalent income levels in the economy in a straightforward way duly recorded. Further he himself has to fix his salary and allowances in the right legal ways. Perhaps, he does not want to change the system as that will take away justification for his colossal wrongs and cornering money in tons.

As part of his strategy he does not permit any controls or regulations on himself. He prevents the growth of all the institutions meant for regulating or cleansing the economic, political and social life. He has successfully prevented establishment of Lokpal for over four decades. The bill has been brought to the Parliament eight times since 1968 and every time it lapsed with the dissolution of the House. He does not want any functional independence for CBI as that will equip the Bureau to pin him and his collaborating bureaucrats down. No wonder, not even one big scam has ever reached the logical end. If in any case some evidence was collected by CBI in any big scam or against a person at high place, it had to make a u-turn and was constrained to change its version as desired from time to time if the government changed or if power equation at centre changed in the same government. This author has depicted such firsthand experiences in detail in his book "*Who Owns CBI: The Naked Truth.*" The issues dealt may be a decade old, but are equally relevant even now as there has been further deterioration since then in place of improvement .

Further, not only the CBI, but the local police also functions completely under his directions. When I.J. Gupta the then Union home minister in 1997 proposed and wanted to discuss the question of separation of investigation from the law and order functions and setting up of State Security Commission in order to eliminate pressure/influence in investigations so that the police could perform its role as envisaged by law without any pressures, every single CM opposed the move fiercely and threatened to boycott the meeting. They feel insecure and incomplete as without this power of moving arm of law used by them in illegal manner for coercion to get people into submission through blackmail and intimidation of opponents, opposition or the dissidents. This power is conferred on police by law in the process of investigation. It is not a secret that the Police is used for illegal purposes day in and day out. Police is made to act as agents of the government, in place of the agents of law. In India rarely, if at all, a police officer can think of working independent of political bosses and their pressures unlike the civilized advanced world. I recall in 1997-98, I was working as Director Research with BPR&D (Bureau of Police Research and Development) in Government of India. A team led by a lady professor from the department of Police studies of a Canadian University visited us. An Assistant Director repeatedly raised the question of relations of Police with the Government or political bosses. She was furious that how could the government interfere in the process of investigation in a civilized country and that it would be an evil day if any politician or anyone else were to exercise control on or interfere in the legal processes that the police perform. Similar sentiment was echoed by Lord Denning, Chief Justice of Great Britain, while commenting on relative roles of Police Commissioner London and the Secretary of states of UK. This very clearly illustrates what the Police are supposed to be like in a sensitive democracy.

> "I have no hesitation, however, in holding that, like every constable in the land he should be, and is, independent of the executive. He is not subject to the orders of the Secretary of State, ...I hold it to be the duty of the Commissioner of Police, as it is of every chief constable, to enforce the law of the land. He must take steps so as to post his men that crimes may be detected; and that honest citizens may go about their affairs in peace. He must decide whether or not suspected persons are to be prosecuted; and, if need be, bring the prosecution or see that it is brought; but in all these things he is not the servant of anyone save of the law itself. No Minister of the Crown can tell him that he must, or must not, keep observations on this place, or that; or that he must, or must not prosecute this man or that one. Nor can any police authority tell him so. The responsibility for law enforcement lies on him. He is answerable to the Law and to the Law alone".

So no one from outside the police department can influence the sacrosanct course of investigation there, but in India the investigating officer keeps on waiting for the directions from the masters and if in some case he takes action as per his conscience and the law that does not suit the political bosses, he would be reprimanded and possibly punished for not having sought instructions in advance.

The politician thereby ensures a position of absolute power for himself, more like a despot and then indulges into corruption and creation of black money while in power and raises voice against all these issues while in opposition.

Politician is not the only person playing dual game. Others also follow the same course for indulging into and justifying corruption by them and their black money. Corruption and black money are basically interwoven. Every group will advocate action against all other groups sparing their own on ground of unavoidable compulsions or harassment to them. They will make anyone believe that they are the holy cows requiring all the protection for their two fold deeds of corruption and hoarding black money/assets. Any action against these holy cows is represented as harassment. That is the argument judges have taken for not declaring their assets and for not submitting to investigations in PF scam. Under public pressure, even though they have agreed partially, but there is a rider that no queries be asked from them as any question or clarification will amount to their harassment.

Whereas transparency about judges is very important as they occupy the nodal position in the system of justice in the country and in particular the criminal justice system as all the agencies dealing with law, have to report all the matters for final adjudication to the courts. Unless judiciary is honest, just, impartial, efficient, fearless and firm, no law enforcing agency will be able to make any dent or take a principled stand for any length of time. The judiciary should be a class by itself in setting standards and in maintaining the same. Our judiciary unfortunately does not qualify these ground level tests. First of all, as stated in details elsewhere, they do not want to declare their assets and want much higher remuneration as their brother advocates earn a lot. In a seminar presided over by Justice JS Varma, the retired Chief Justice of India in the Institute for Social Sciences at New Delhi, a very senior Supreme Court advocate Rajiv Dhawan spoke for higher remuneration to the members of Judiciary to bring them closer to what they earn as practising advocates as their earnings decline steeply when they leave their practice to join the bench. With a twinkle in his eyes, he also mentioned that on this meagre salary they have to pay heavy tax as well. The reference and the implications were plain and obvious that as advocates they evade the income tax. Everybody laughed as it is well known that most of the lawyers like many of the other professionals issue receipt only for a nominal amount and bulk of their earnings are thus in the unaccounted sector. Is this the reason that as judges they do not want to disclose their assets and do not want to entertain any query or question as the skeletons of their undeclared or under declared incomes or benami transactions since their days as advocates will tumble down. Could this be the reason why our judiciary does not take the white collar crime, the tax evasion and corruption so seriously? Do they see their own reflection in some way or the other in the persons accused of such crimes? As human beings, their judgments naturally will have to be conditioned and coloured by their mindset, which in turn depends upon their background particularly for integrity and respect for law. Those who join from legal/judicial services are judged for their suitability, both for their professional skills and capabilities as also for their integrity, but there does not seem to be any objective mechanism of ascertaining the integrity and efficiency, over a period, of the candidates under consideration for joining as judges from the bar. It is in this perspective that, because of lack of information, the Supreme Court collegiums recommended the case of Dinakaran for elevation to the apex court.

Further, the judiciary does not allow anyone to peep into their closed door affairs. In U.P., PF case, the Supreme Court itself bent the law when they asked the investigating officer not to interrogate the hon'ble judges, but only to frame a questionnaire, get it approved from the apex court and seek response from the judges on the same. The investigating officer will take it as a clear hint that no action is to be taken and in any case by itself it was enough to pressurize him to refrain from straight investigations. This is the sort of pressure and privileged treatment the politician and the other influential groups claim and exercise on him. The judges might justify that they were possibly following their own decision in Veeraswamy case, but that should have no relevance in this case when preliminary enquiry had already been conducted by a judicial officer, Rama Jain under the orders of the High Court. Also, that the judgment in the Veeraswamy case by itself was controversial. The mind of the investigating officer gets so set that he views such pressures as another misappropriation of a privilege by the persons in authority, the judges this time. The enquiry by Rama Jain had collected specific and detailed evidence from records and indicted them all. After that enquiry report, they were all reduced to the status of the accused persons in a criminal case. An accused is only an accused and enjoys no perk or privilege under the law, then why discrimination. In all fairness, all these judges irrespective of the court they belong to, should have been taken off the court work with immediate effect. If, however, the judiciary feels that the sitting judges should not be examined as that will cause some sort of demoralization or embarrassment, then let all these 36 judges resign and vacate their positions. All other public servants so involved are placed under suspension so that they are not able to exercise influence and indulge into objectionable activities any more. There is no reason why they should continue to preside over their respective courts and also why they should not have been interrogated, searched, arrested and chargesheeted as per the evidence and the requirement of law instead of trampling the law of the land. Is the principle "Be you ever so high, the law is above you", only to be quoted in the judgments and not to be upheld and much less to be followed in the case of the judicial officers or the other influential people.

Similarly, nobody is allowed to examine the judicial delays. The judicial officers continue to function under a particular mindset and disallow any fresh air by way of research that is so essential for any progress or any change. Following the 120th report of the Law Commission, their chorus is to increase the number of judges in proportion to the population on the scale prevalent in the USA. The Commission itself was not fully convinced of the criterion that they recommended, but now the judiciary has made it a prestige point. They are not prepared to look into adjournments, stays, and bails etc. that cause delays. I happened to be in Mumbai in November 2008. A news item appeared in the *Mumbai Mail* that a young boy who was arrested on charge of a small theft, had been languishing in jail for the past eleven months. This time on 5th November, when he appeared before the metropolitan magistrate for 24th time, he was again remanded to judicial custody as he had no one to stand surety for him. The boy himself had been requesting for his trial and for deciding his case so that he could undergo the punishment and get out of jail as he had already spent more time than the normal punishment awarded for such a trivial matter. He was so disgusted that in the open court he threw his *Chappal* on the judge. Even if the judge spent 5 minutes each time in his case, the total time spent without any useful purpose was 120 minutes, whereas the judge would not have taken more than 30 minutes in hearing the case and passing the judgment. Apart from keeping him in unnecessary confinement, has the judge in question not wasted 90 minutes of the court time enough for deciding another three such cases? The inefficiency of court kept this young man in wrongful confinement but no one can question their ways. There is general pendency of cases and it is well known that judicial procedures are mainly responsible for that, but no scientific study by experts from outside is allowed and the emphasis is on adding to the number of judges. I have nothing against increasing the number of judges, but it has to follow some criterion of workload and incidentally the workload of an Indian judge is much lighter in terms of disposal of number of cases that come to the share of each judge on the basis of average annual cases as compared to a US judge. The out of place comparisons are drawn so as to retain their privileges intact and add to perks and compensation without any reference to the number of cases disposed of by them and their counterparts in those countries and particularly in the USA.

Civil servant arrogates hidden perks, cooperates and collaborates with the people in power to commit all the indiscretions and then seeks refuge from law. There are a number of straight forward, well meaning officers who are persons of integrity, but they are sidelined. The above is a sad commentary on the functioning of officers in general. It is they who persuaded the politician to issue and enforce the infamous single directive, convincing and assuring the politician that once no enquiries can be conducted against them, they will be able to carry out his bidding better. Single directive provided that without permission of the government, no enquiry or investigation can be undertaken against any officer of and above the rank of Joint Secretary to Government of India and government normally had been declining such permission. This issue became a focal point in the Jain Hawala case and in December, 1997 the Supreme Court ruled this order to be discriminatory and ultra-vires the constitution. Lo and behold, only a little later, an ordinance was brought giving legal status to this provision. There was sharp criticism in media and public leading to withdrawal of the order. But see the impunity and contempt for public opinion as against personal protection of perks and privileges that soon the bureaucracy found a way out and quietly included it in the CVC Act, though it had no relevance for that Act.

Prosecution sanction is another privilege. Under the law of corruption, no case can be chargesheeted without permission from the executive irrespective of what the evidence could be. It is another privilege continuing from the colonial days when Britishers had to overlook the indiscretion by the officers committed to British Empire in order to oblige them and get their unquestioned loyalty.

Businessmen often blame their own corruption on the government agencies arguing "How can we be expected to uphold integrity when we have to pay our way to get our legitimate works done from the departments/ agencies of the government?" They are not entirely wrong, but at the same time they bribe to get bigger advantages as Hyderabad Economic Committee Report observed as early as 1948 "....the rich man will not pay unless he gets some return and the poor except under duress." Businessmen may have compulsions sometime but every time he is a collaborator sharing the booty. He has also invented his defence mechanism. It is he who got FERA changed into FEMA for his own protection. Besides, being custodian of money he buys his way through and arrogates all the perks and privileges enjoyed by other elite groups.

The process has been taken to the extreme in certain other cases where either the law itself was changed or its edges were blunted. If FERA had the punch that primarily pinched the business and industry, they got it changed to FFMA removing the criminal element from the violation. Now it is a civil matter. Apart from making immediate investigations almost impossible in the country, it has far reaching implications that the tax havens will not entertain any request from India in connection with offences related to foreign exchange as that ceases to be a criminal offence and unless it is a criminal offence in India, they are not obliged to entertain any request even for parting with any information under the International Laws; cooperation in investigations or repatriating the black money kept with them, remains a far cry.

Further, the law relating to Benami property is a glaring example of how protective shield is created by the elite around themselves. Benami Transactions Act was enacted in 1988, but despite lapse of two decades the rules have not been framed and the law as such cannot be put into action without rules being in place. Reverting to the law, the offence is non-cognizable and bailable. Even when the law becomes operational, the CBI or any other agency would not be able to register a case and undertake investigations. It will have to file a complaint in the court that only will decide what action is to be taken. The interval occupied by such proceedings will allow enough time for the accused to set his house in order, come clean and threaten the complainant and the CBI with defamation and damages.

Blocking of the Lokpal Bill for over four decades presents the most brazen behaviour on the part of the politician in the process to protect himself from any enquiries by an agency outside the government. All over the world, the Ombudsman is a recognized institution since ages. India also proposed an Ombudsman called Lokpal and a bill to that effect was introduced in the Parliament in 1968, but it was not passed and lapsed with the dissolution of the House on completion of its term. The process has been repeated in every Parliament after that (except the last House), but the bill is never taken up after its introduction in the House and has been lapsing with completion of the term of the House. The shade of the government or the party has made no difference. It is obvious how afraid the political class is of this bill as Lokpal will have a right to undertake impartial enquiries *suo motto,* no wonder our politicians dread that.

Non-ratification of the UNCAC (United Nations Convention Against Corruption) for the last six years is an insurmountable obstacle making any investigations abroad meaningless rather impossible. In 2003, the UNO realizing the damage the corruption was causing particularly to the lower sections of the poor countries, deliberated and enacted the above convention in order to promote cooperation between various countries to fight against corruption. The parties to the convention are obliged to extend all the help in investigations in their respective countries and in particular in chasing the funds parked abroad. India had signed the treaty in 2003, but it has still to be ratified by the Parliament. The ratification is scrupulously being avoided so that the investigating agencies cannot enlist any help from abroad and solve the cases. This impinges on our nation in two ways. First, if the treaty were in place, many cases could be worked out as the participating countries will be obliged to extend help. That could be a positive step in bringing our wealth from tax havens. Actually the convention is a very good document at cleansing and in particular strengthening the institutions fighting against corruption. Relevant extracts from the treaty have been compiled in annexure-"E". Article 6(2) of the convention clearly lays down that the enforcement agencies will have to be given complete independence, meaning thereby that the CBI and all such agencies will have to be given complete freedom at par with the international standards as enjoyed by the FBI of USA, ICAC of Hong Kong or Australia. Not only that, article 36 of the convention grants similar independence to other specialized agencies that take part in fight against corruption. It is a well known fact that the governments in India whether Central or state have been resisting free investigations and have not yielded even an inch in relaxing their complete control, direction and continue to manipulate investigations as ever. If the convention is signed, that will provide not only further aid to investigation, but change the scenario take away the interference, free the mindset of the investigator and make him answerable to law in place of executive or political bosses. As per article 43(2) of the convention, the doctrine of dual criminality "in matters of international cooperation wherever dual criminality is considered a requirement, it shall be deemed fulfilled irrespective of whether the laws of the requested state party place the offence within the same category of offence or dominate the offence by the same terminology as the requesting state". Further article 43 clause 8 lays down *"state parties shall not decline to render mutual legal assistance pursuant to this article on the ground of bank security"*. The ratification of the convention will loosen the absolute hold of the government by granting independence of action to various agencies and that leading to facilitation of information from abroad even to the extent of relaxing the banking secrecy and dual criminality. The elite of all the categories in India will dread that day as it will amount to signing their own death warrant. No wonder, the governments of different shades have refrained from ratifying the treaty, nor will they venture whatever the Prime Minister may talk about fighting corruption or its zero tolerance level. The elite will not permit and hold him back irrespective of his intentions. It is for this sordid reason that India is constrained to hold back the ratification, despite the fact that we signed the treaty as early as in 2003.The internal compulsions are always more pressing. The insiders confide that this is the main cause of worry. The government with great care and caution has been keeping CBI under tabs, but once the treaty is ratified and the stipulated independence is granted, the tabs would disappear making the life of the elite very tough. By refusing to ratify, the intentions of the government have been clear to the international community as well, that India does not intend to fight corruption and much less to bring the money back from tax havens. Secondly, the message goes the world over that we also do not intend to take fight against corruption seriously.

This is reflected on the ground in the way we handled the LGT affair that presents a shameless account. The Germans were willing and had offered to give the names of the Indians maintaining secret accounts in Liechtenstein, but we did not move to obtain the names or details. When the public pressure mounted, the government had no option but to apply. However, when the names have been obtained, these are not being made public. Opposition is also not making any issue. People have started talking and believing that since politicians of all the shades, along with the bureaucrats and businessmen across the spectrum are involved, so every elite group is interested in keeping the names under secrecy.

Every group has been opposing the idea of declaring its assets. When on public demand and on court orders on a PIL it became unavoidable to file statement of assets alongwith the nomination papers, the politician fumed and fretted, but saved the situation for himself as Election Commission does not have power to test the veracity of the declaration. It thus remains more of a formality for him, but it is a real big beginning as people themselves will start investigating their assets in due course. Coming back to the judiciary; it is intriguing how can the same judiciary that made declaration mandatory for the politician, skirt the issue and avoid declaration when it comes to them. It may appear that the politician is now taking his turn to compel the judiciary. If it is so it is welcome as healthy competition at cleansing each other. Judges feel it infra-*dig* to file the property return and also fear harassment. If at all they have to file returns, they want no further queries or enquiries i.e. whatever they declare should summarily be just kept on record. If so, where is the need for this at all? It is all a cover, a shield that they are taking on to protect themselves. If it is harassment then all others are also equally harassed by this very step, then why single out the judges alone? They should be more transparent than anyone else as Ceaser's wife has to be the fairest of all. Legally, as public servants they are also covered along with others and are obliged to declare their assets. In view of a number of instances of judiciary that came to light in the recent past, latest being the UP PF case and now Dinakaran case, there is hardly any justification for any differential treatment to judiciary. Basically, in view of the exalted position of the judiciary, the self control, the discipline and the exposition of any wrong deed by a member of the fraternity, should be much stern, thorough and quick. Civil servants do file returns though not regularly. They adjust filing with bungling they commit and then choose their time to file or not to file. The eternal excuse of being over busy is evergreen for cover up. No doubt all the corrupt elements oppose declaration of assets.

Exemption from RTI is a similar privilege that all these sections have tried to claim. One wonders, if in democracy people are the masters, how anyone of the servants, right upto the President can hide himself/herself from the view of the masters, be it judiciary, executive or the political leadership. There are situations of national interest that have been included for exemptions in the Act, but there cannot be any relaxation from RTI for any group from the general principle as any relaxation will be for hiding their own weaknesses or misconduct repugnant to the public interest. There could be some reasons or circumstances for exemption from/relaxation in RTI, but there cannot be a single case for exemption/ relaxation from declaration of assets or operation of the Corruption related Acts.

5

Tax Havens and Money Stashed Abroad

We have seen in the previous chapters how mills are working overtime to generate black money/incomes. Insignificant industries and sectors of economic activity are evading large sums as taxes and concealing the amounts of income beyond imagination. This slush has been partly kept in cash and partly in the form of other assets, both movable and immovable inside the country and the other part is sent abroad by the people of substance who have the right connections abroad. The practice has been continuing since pre-independence days. It is unfortunate that freedom made no difference to this drain of the nation. Rather, it took turn for the worse as the state expanded its activity in the field of economic development. Spending by the state went up and so did the corruption and the evasion of taxes, both of which soared steeply imparting proportionate push to the deposits in banks abroad. Slush that reached abroad was thought to be safe beyond the reach of Indian Enforcement agencies and keeps accumulating there into hefty accounts. Further, the elite required black money abroad to finance their luxurious living on their visits to various foreign lands, as also for education of their children in foreign countries. Indians are known to spend a lot when on visits abroad. They are classed as the best spenders clubbed with the tourists from the rich US. It is also well known that they would make heavy purchases of the items of luxury that were not available here and at that time nor was their import allowed legally. They brought them home that too without paying import duties. It was clear cut smuggling in reality. What to speak of the people from business, industry or political fields, even the officers and ministers of government that too known for their good reputation for highest integrity indulged in this smuggling activity. I recall an incident of around 1973 that I watched first hand. An officer of the level of additional secretary to the Government of India had gone abroad on a private visit. When he was about to return, he specially summoned one of his subordinate senior officer back from far off interiors in Himalayas to Delhi. A batch mate of this officer was said to be the collector customs at Delhi Airport and the officer was to liaise with him in order to arrange the passage of the top officer through the customs check uninterrupted so that all the goods that he brought, passed the customs check without payment of any duties. The ostensible reason circulated for calling him back to Delhi was to avoid harassment to the top officer at the hands of the customs officials. It was, however, learnt that the officer had evaded taxes. It was nothing unusual and no eyebrows were raised by those who learnt about the incident as that was the accepted norm that most of the officers and politicians followed. The businessmen and the industrialist bribed their way through, but most of them also evaded the taxes. It was thought to be a perk and a privilege of the senior civil servants and the political bosses. So open was the system that the officer who had made all the arrangements, himself narrated this to me without any compunction. This top senior officer was otherwise a person of known impeccable integrity that however, did not suffer for evading taxes. That unfortunately has been the concept of integrity of the senior civil servants as also the mindset of the entire spectrum of Indian Elite, who, barring some honourable exceptions, have by and large, evaded all sorts of taxes, indulged into corrupt practices and black money operations ever since the independence.

More recent case of 1995 of the Union Minister Kamal Nath shows how the honest customs officer was harassed and punished for her audacity to ask for payment of due tax. On his return from abroad he did not declare any dutiable item in his declaration and as usual for the VIPs, left the airport asking his staff to collect the baggage. Unfortunately for him a straightforword, non-obliging and non-bending Deputy Collector R Shakuntala was posted there, who evaluated and imposed duty alongwith penalty for false declaration. The minister was furious and she was immediately hourided out of Delhi. The then Finance Minister who was none other than the present PM Manmohan Singh remained a helpless silent spectator. The powerful politician had shot down the law, dwarfed all the enforcement and upheld the evasion of tax by himself.

Further, the delivery of hush money that accrues out of the import/export affairs or out of kick-backs is preferably taken abroad and is naturally held in the safety and secrecy of bank accounts there. The extent of money stashed abroad ultimately depends upon the quantum of generation of unaccounted income. There can be no exact and authentic estimate with proof of the amount of either the tax evasion or the generation of black money or of the deposits held abroad. It can only be assessed approximately with the help of collateral or secondary evidence as has been worked out in Chapter II.

The money siphoned abroad must bear some ratio to the taxes evaded and the income cornered into the blind alleys. We have seen in the earlier chapter that the tax evasion is to the extent of Rs. 27.6 lac crores every year and cumulative tax evasion on the recorded incomes since 1950-51 has been to the tune of Rs. 150 lac crores at the current price level and when unrecorded incomes are also clubbed, that is the black economy is also taken into account, the total evasion mounts to Rs. 450 lac crores. The Black incomes generated would be further much more at least 2-3 times, placing the cumulative conversion of black income between Rs. 900 lac crores and Rs. 1350 lac crores ($20 to 30 trillion), a part of it would have been consumed over the years, a part might be held in cash, and the remainder would have been converted into various assets and a substantial portion of it siphoned abroad to the tax havens. A part of this money would also have been consumed or invested side by side abroad and the remaining held as deposits. The exact amount of black money held in secret accounts could be anybody's guess. The analysis, however, has shown that out of huge black money, a figure of even $ 7to 8 trillion stashed abroad is quite plausible.

Looking from another angle, a study was conducted by Professor John Zdanowicz and others of Florida International University, Miami, for the year 1993-94. The *Hindustan Times* reporting on the study mentioned, "India charged 200 times less for selling its exercise cycles to the US. The similar concession for industrial miners diamonds was 100 times less, for unworked diamonds nearly 120 times less, storage batteries 40 per cent less and regulators were found underpriced to the extent of 30 times". On the other hand, the picture was just the opposite in case of exports from the USA to India, "if in a unit-form US sold tetracycline at 11.74 per gram to other countries, the rate was 1102.50 per gram for India... for video cassette recording India paid 40 times higher, for chlorine India paid over 22 times higher." Alarming indeed!

The study repeated for 1994 and 1995, reported in the *Times of India* disclosed similar facts and estimated the maximum and the minimum losses that might have been caused to the economy through the dual processes placing the capital flight i.e. losses caused to India at a minimum of 20 per cent on imports and 40 per cent on exports. The USA is among cleaner countries in the field of international trade as compared to others. Even if the same percentage is extended to trade with other countries, India thus lost more than its annual balance of trade deficit on this score. As per *Economic Survey 2008-09* Indian exports were \$168.7 billion and imports \$ 287.7 billion. Extending the same rates for the year 2008-09, the annual losses will amount to \$67.5 billion and \$ 57.5 billion respectively. In total, the country might have lost \$125.0 billion or Rs. 5.62 lac crores against a balance of trade deficit of Rs.5.36 lac crores. It is mind boggling and beyond comprehension that the country is being cheated to that extent annually in the form of foreign exchange. I dread to compute the losses that have been caused since 1950-51, though the statistics for the period are available.

Raymond Baker of Global Financial Integrity, the organization spearheading the US campaign against the tax havens, regards the international trade as the biggest spinner of black money. He estimates that 30 percent of the illicit money comes out of the organized crime like the drug trade etc., 5 percent is the contribution of corruption and the remaining 65 percent is born out of the international trade. It is a different matter that corruption ultimately sustains the entire edifice though by itself it may be negligible.

It is in view of this fact that the USA is contemplating to bring a legislation to make it mandatory to follow international norm of pricing in imports and exports and the banks clearing the payments are proposed to be empowered to verify and certify so that the custom duty or the VAT or the income tax are not evaded in either of the two countries.

The countries of the third world suffer heavily on this account as it causes a great drain on their economies and they have no option but to borrow heavily from abroad. If only the outflow of their resources could be checked, some of the countries of the third world, like India, may have enough of foreign exchange resources and may not borrow from abroad at all. After all, as per Raymond Baker during the decade of 90s the aid given by the advanced countries to the poor nations averaged to $ 80 bn. as against an average flight of $800 bn. out of these third world countries. Incidentally our own annual losses in international trade are to the extent of $125 bn. as worked out above for 2008-09. Switzerland remains the roof and crown of the slush parks though many new centres have also emerged. No wonder Switzerland has the second highest per capita income in the world, with its banking industry in the lead. This drain from the third world will continue unabated unless certain structural changes are brought about in the secrecy covering such banks all over the world.

Various estimates of accumulated black money of Indians held abroad have appeared from time to time as some information keeps leaking from the primary sources to the press. The latest estimate in current circulation is that the Swiss Banks have a total of $2.15 trillion in secret accounts in Switzerland of which $1.456 trillion belong to Indians. That constitutes a very high share of 60 percent of the total. There are also Swiss banks operating beyond the boundaries of Switzerland. Earlier revelations in 1996 imputed to a Swiss bank Director had placed the magnitude of money kept by Indians in Swiss bank accounts as large as $2.55 trillion, which normally should have doubled during these 13 years, whereas, *prima facie*, it appears to have shrunk. There are some reasons for this fall also. First, that the number of tax havens that used to be just around a dozen in 1996, has multiplied to over six dozens. Some of the money could have moved to these new places. Second, in the din created by the strong action of IRS of USA and the subsequent court cases that are still under hearing, an uncertainty has gripped the depositors, who have every reason to move away their funds to other available tax havens. Third, a very large section in India believes that bulk of the FDI that has come to India, emanates from this very money that was stashed abroad by Indians and the same is being brought duly laundered through Mauritius and such like other channels. No wonder the FDI received through Mauritius route during 2007-09 is placed as high as Rs. 124000 crores (or $275 billion). Naturally, there is a corresponding fall in the holding of Indians in Swiss banking system as also in other tax havens. Holdings with Swiss banking chain might have declined, but that does not mean that Indian holdings of black money abroad have declined to the extent it appears on the surface. The Hasan Ali phenomenon is a pointer to the contrary.

Hassan Ali is a stud farm operator of Pune. His lid was blown off by the Enforcement Directorate/Income tax department. The Enforcement Directorate detected an account of Hassan Ali with Swiss banking giant UBS, having a balance of 8.1 billion dollars. It has reliably been learnt that the account disclosed credits being received from various sources including the international arms dealers, indicating that perhaps he is keeping funds on behalf of certain other people. As a stud farm operator or just a Hawala dealer by himself he is a small fry. He is the repository of the money of some big people. But on the other hand, Hassan Ali cannot be a single such person. There would be very many such persons in this country of over 112 crore souls who have similar accounts abroad on behalf of other biggies. If there are just 1000 Indians holding accounts comparable to that of Hassan Ali, only their total amount in secret accounts would be of the order of $ 8000 billion or 8 trillion dollars or Rs. 400 lac crores and not just the bare $ 1456 billion or Rs.70 lac crores. The reasons why the figures given out by the Swiss banks could have fallen to 1456 billion dollars since the decade of 90s, have been explained above. Finally, they may not be divulging truth and might be underplaying in the wake of stiff US action against the Swiss banks. Even otherwise, the latest total estimates of black money in the world in all the tax havens combined now are being placed around 11700 billion dollars by the Tax Justice Network. If the same percentage of 60 that has been circulating widely, holds good for the share of Indians in the total deposits in all the tax havens, the total of black money held by Indians in various tax havens thus would work out to 7020 billion or 7.2 trillion dollars which appears to be more accurate and more realistic in the light of the Hassan Ali story. We may look from any angle the black money held by Indians in the country and abroad is just mind-boggling. If only the Indian wealth lying there can be brought home, we will turn into one of the top rich nations on the globe.

6

Bringing back the Black Money from Tax Havens

Shock waves jolted the nation when the mega figures of money of Indians held in secret bank accounts abroad were projected during the election campaign for Union Parliament in May 2009. The issues that particularly agitated the people were the enormity of Indian money coupled with absolute lack of efforts for recovering it, contrasted with the efforts put in by USA for recovering their much smaller amount and their successfully curbing of objectionable Swiss Bank activities. At that very time the Germans exposed and curbed the LGT activities successfully. LGT is the bank of Liechtenstein, a small principality of 35000 people on the German border. The principal vocation of its people is in the secrecy of its banking. However, Germany won over one of its employees and obtained a pen drive containing information about all the secret accounts with the bank. The information disclosed the names of not only the German citizens, but also from other nations around the world including India. Germans offered to disclose the names of various account holders to their respective countries if the latter made a formal request for the same. Such offer came to India as well. Against that background there was complete absence of any response from our own government. The middle and lower classes were deeply wounded that the higher sections have deprived them of their dues and transported the money abroad. After all, it is a problem created by one to two percent or at the most five percent of the population that constitute the higher echelons of the society. So the response of the public was spontaneous when one party gave the call that they will bring the money back in 100 days if they were voted to power. No doubt it was election time rhetoric as nobody will or can bring back the money in just 100 days. Even a decade would be too short a period for the recall of this money as the problems involved are immense. There are legal issues, issues of international relations and many more including the local laws of our country as also of that country. But then a beginning has to be made which has not happened and nor will anything ordinarily happen, as the elite understandably put up very stiff resistance and the reins of nation are in their hands. The nation is placed in a very unenviable situation.

If USA could get its funds back from Switzerland, that too with penalty, their case is different. Their standard of morality and nationalist spirit is at much higher a level. The services are far better professionalized and the co-efficient of corruption is much lower as compared to India. They could project and press their case whereas we are still fumbling over the LGT affair despite an offer from the German government, what to speak of the Swiss banks. Further USA is the world leader and not only the economic superpower who could otherwise also compel anybody for that matter. At the top of it, they have spared no effort in pursuing their cases and treated their tax evaders as criminals along with their bankers who conspired or abetted. India should have the requisite will supported by serious actions.

The problem has to be tackled on two fronts. First, the money stashed abroad has to be brought back and second, further evasion of taxes and conversion of incomes into the black stream has to be prevented. Bringing back the black money from abroad will not be easy. Unless pressurized and compelled, the banks that park the slush will not cooperate and the depositors from India will also oppose any such move tooth and nail. When in view of hue and cry by public during elections, the government is reported to have raised this question with the Swiss Bank authorities; the latter raised the technical issue of double taxation. It is only one of the preliminary objections, many more such and other objections can be expected as Swiss economy is heavily dependent on secret accounts. It may take years to execute a new treaty, if at all it happens. All these banks and the financial institutions are enjoying the fruits of interest-free deposits and in certain cases may even be charging maintenance fee for keeping secrecy. They will not give up the goose that lays the golden eggs. Something may be expected to happen under the intense international pressure only, but one can be sure that by that time the deposits would have been moved to some other destinations. Reasonably, one should not pin much hope on the recovery of this vast chunk of wealth particularly in the immediate future, though there should be no laxity in the efforts as that only will pressurize and dissuade the depositors as also the slush banker and prevent further flight of our money abroad. This chapter deals with bringing back the deposits from abroad and the next is devoted to stop the very generation and hence the drain of the slush altogether.

For bringing back this enormous amount of money, all out sincere efforts are needed. It would be a long protracted war. As a first step, the banking secrecy has to go, but it is doubtful if our government will take any initiative towards this end as is obvious from the cold response on part of the government in LGT affair, despite the fact that the Transparency International India had at that time exposed how the Indian Government was not seeking information from the German Government about billions of dollars of unaccounted money that belonged to the people of India, lying in Liechtenstein. A number of other countries like USA, Finland, Norway, Sweden, Canada, Italy, U.K and Ireland whose nationals were also included in the same list, seriously collected the information about their citizens. While dealing with the issue of Indian money in Swiss banks, I had visualized such situation long back and had foreseen this attitude of the Government dominated by the same elite who keep such slush, pointing out clearly in my book, *Who Owns CBI: The Naked Truth,* that "....it will not be easy to take any step in this direction, as the first obstacle would come from Indian elites, holding such accounts/assets abroad; who will oppose any such move tooth and nail. But no meaningful fight against corruption, black money and plethora of economic offences can be really successful without such radical measures."

Banking Secrecy Laws Abroad

It is the banking secrecy that makes hiding and keeping slush funds possible. As such the Swiss banks and their likes have a very prominent role in facilitating and perpetuating corruption by guaranteeing enjoyment of its fruit through their secrecy. Kickbacks are often credited into accounts abroad to avoid detection. Money, duly laundered, may sometimes be brought back to India through normal banking channels, by showing it as gift from some relative or friend, or simply the payment earned through exports. These days laundering centers like Mauritius have sprung up and India is said to be receiving back its own money in form of FDI. Even if it is argued that money is flowing back, still the exchequer loses the tax and now has to shell out various concessions on this so called FDI. Meenakshi Rao outlines the mechanism of the laundering centrs like Mauritius in her article "Slush Slush" in *Pioneer* dated 15 March 2009 observes: "According to a report in Le Monde, one of the biggest foreign investors in India is Mauritius. The report quotes Kannan Privanisavan, professor at Melbourne, to detail this strange phenomenon. *The maharajas invested their fortune in London, as they have always done. The nouveau riche and many of the firms continue to place, either legally or illegally, their profits in such banks. From there, the money sets off again on a long circuit which arrives at Mauritius, the little paradise. Then, under falsified identities of their true owners, the money re-enters India without being taxed.*

The most popular route is through hawala channels though corporates often take the easier and more undetectable route of under-invoicing exports and over-invoicing imports." The select few Indian citizens continue to bleed the nation dry in collusion with global tax havens which have earned the tag of being parasitical. As of now, there are a plethora of ways that the rogue citizens have been employing to get their money deposited illegally in secret accounts abroad.

In my own way, I had raised this issue and tried to analyse how to tackle this problem in my article titled "Need for sustained efforts to combat corruption" in the *Tribune* dated 27.7.2003, written in context of the Eleventh International Anti-Corruption Conference held at Seoul, that itself had resolved that corruption should be designated as a crime against humanity. It criticised the doctrine of affording immunity from extradition to those accused of corruption and stressed the need for a code of conduct for the judiciary.

The circumstances have undergone a change the world over because of the actions of IRS of USA and compulsions of various countries in the face of depression and the consequent encomic difficulties. The mighty countries are now working hard to evolve systems and create mechanisms at the international level for effective cooperation in this fight as the tax havens with their deep vested interests have been trying to protect their empires.

For the first time, the Swiss banking secrecy has been challenged by the Internal Revenue Service of the USA and also it was the first time ever that the secrecy of any such bank was broken by the Germans in case of LGT. An encouraging aspect was that the German government was prepared to cooperate and give the information on demand to every other country as well. This was a God sent opportunity as normally the banking authorities and the national governments there do not cooperate and rather create all sorts of obstacles and make it impossible even to know the holdings of our citizens with them. However the slush money arising out of drug trade had been treated differently. If it is suspected that the money in a bank has some relation with the drug trade, the secrecy laws stand automatically relaxed, as these have been amended to that extent. It was done on insistence of the big western powers, as drugs have been their problem. After attack on World Trade Centre in New York on 11th September 2001, the money held by terrorists has also been frozen. For countries like India, all economic offenders including the corrupt Indians as also the cooperating Swiss-bankers, are the 'Financial Terrorists' or their harbourers. The major problem of the third world is corruption, and the secrecy laws aid and abet it. It would not be an exaggeration to say that the people of countries like Switzerland are more like receivers of stolen property, leading parasitic existence. This hypocrisy does not go well with their famed high stance on morality. They should abandon such laws and throw their banking business open and transparent. India should take up this question with Swiss banks, the western world and with all possible international organizations, including the U N, OECD etc. The countries of the third world, and India in particular, should also join them in their crusade and agitate for abrogation of banking secrecy laws.

It may be argued that the banks cannot make the accounts of their customers public, as confidentiality of finances of any individual is of the greatest essence and should be maintained thoroughly. Here distinction should be drawn between the confidentiality and the secrecy. The limit of legitimate confidentiality ends, the moment the details of an account or of an individual are required by the nodal investigating agency of the country of which the individual is a citizen.

The World is Serious Now

The world over efforts are afoot, both severally as also collectively, by most of the advanced countries to control the activities of the tax havens that have already taken heavy toll of their resources and prosperity. It is unfortunate that India, the most affected country of the world, not only by the highest sheer volume of its slush, but also in view of the fact that we are the biggest poor country of the world has taken no steps whatsoever. Operations of black money save taxes for the richer classes, but cause a heavy strain on the poorer sections down the line by further pushing up the tax rates that becomes necessary to mop up resources at a minimum level.

UK, availing the offer from Germany, has already obtained the names and accounts of its defaulter citizens from LGT and has already imposed penalties on them. Such actions create a salutary effect as having paid penalty; they have lost the incentive to keep these funds abroad and will naturally bring the same back home on their own. At the same time it acts as a deterrent for others from carting their funds abroad to these tax havens. We could also have proceeded straight to German government, availed their open offer some two years back and acted against the defaulters, recovering straight the due taxes with the maximum possible penalties without waiting whether these funds are brought back or not. Lately we are supposed to have obtained the names, but the same have been kept secret without any reason or any apparent action against any defaulter despite the lapse of quite a few months. On the one hand we are fighting against the Secrecy, but on the other we are also practising the same. If only stiff penalties had been imposed and recovered they would themselves have got back the funds from LGT.

Australia has already asked the Swiss banks to give out the details of its citizens on the same lines on which the Swiss banks had released the details of 4450 accounts of US nationals to their Internal Revenue Service. The Australian government must be having some particulars of involvement of their citizens in criminal or some other objectionable activities that are held admissible by the Swiss authorities, so their request has been entertained. Unfortunately, we are lacking the stern laws that are required and whatever provisions we have are stonewalled by our feudal mindset that restrains the enforcement agencies from taking any cognizance against the big people occupying high places. If we cannot bring such misconduct under the ambit of laws in our own country and if we cannot initiate any action, our demand on other countries will naturally be treated by them as witch –hunt or the fishing expedition as the Swiss authorities actually rebuffed us recently.

Some of the countries have resorted to direct action. France, for instance has closed down all the branches of its banking system in these tax havens. USA has enacted laws like "Stop Tax Haven`s Abuse Act" for deterring the use of offshore secrecy jurisdictions for tax evasion. It stipulates certain presumptions in tax proceedings so as to meet with the bank secrecy laws that put the onus to prove that his transactions are bonafides and lawful on the account holder in the tax haven. The Act also provides stiff penalties upto $1 million per violation of US security laws on public companies or their officers, directors or major shareholders along with recovery of 150 percent of the amount carted to such accounts.

Apart from these efforts at individual level, UK, France and Germany have decided to pool together to finish all the tax havens by 2010. Besides, the OECD has been engaged in serious efforts in controlling the fall out of the tax havens. OECD has been regularly monitoring the activities of the tax havens. It blacklists the uncooperative ones and singles them out for action.

G-20, a group of 20 nations all over the globe, is making its own efforts and by 2010 wants to pass an Act for Elimination of Tax Havens and completely implement the same by 2012. If they succeed, the tax havens would be finished in their context. India is also a member of G-20 group, but we need associate more actively and be a party to this enactment and should not opt out through the back door as we did in the case of UNCAC. We signed that treaty in 2003, but have not ratified it till this day. Not only our reputation for seriously fighting against corruption has taken a beating, but also we have lost on other counts that the treaty offers. Apart from getting cooperation at the international level, the treaty confers the benefit of certain presumptions that make investigation abroad possible and makes cooperation by other signatories mandatory in fields like affording exemption from the doctrine of dual criminality and even the provisions of banking secrecy under article 43 of the treaty.

Further, a number of countries have signed the "Tax Information Exchange agreements" with various tax havens and about a dozen countries have signed/initiated such agreements with Swiss banks. These also include some of the African countries as well, but not India. The idea was developed by the OECD Global Forum on Effective Exchange of Information so as to avoid harmful tax practices as the Centre for Tax Policy and Administration, an organ of OECD itself dealing with the subject observed, "Exchange of information is an important tool in fighting non-compliance with the tax laws in an increasingly borderless world."

Besides, they have also encouraged certain NGOs and independent study groups to monitor, research, gauge the extent of the problem, suggest solutions and follow up the whole issues within and outside the countries. Global Financial Integrity of USA, Tax Justice Network of UK, the Tax Policy and Administration and the Transparency and Exchange of Information for Tax Purposes, of OECD are some of the organizations that provide a framework for in-depth monitoring various tax havens as also the tax evaders. They are doing real useful work, study the problems in details, suggest corrective measures against the aberrations and follow up the issues to their logical end. In USA, the Global Financial Integrity was closely associated with IRS in the court trial in cases arising out of their investigations into the activities of the Swiss banks. It is partly due to the hard-line taken and the support extended by the GFI that IRS could stand firm and that compelled the UBS to give out details of 4450 accounts alongwith paying a penalty of $ 780 million, a big achievement. Similar actions are being taken by quite a few more organizations in many countries of the world but somehow we in India have lagged behind and not done anything substantial at all.

Assets Owned Abroad

Apart from bank accounts, there is another dimension that the black money is kept in the form of property or some other assets that could be acquired abroad. Since the agency of one country cannot conduct investigations in another country, some rules need to be framed so that the particulars of deposits or of properties held abroad could be known to the mother country, in the name of whose citizens these may stand. In countries like USA and most of the major European countries, the records of registry are open documents and there is no problem in obtaining them, but we have made no effort at acquiring this open data. It hardly requires a mention that a large number of Indian citizens own undeclared properties there, the legitimate presumption is that the same were acquired by the black money. Indian embassy could easily collect such actionable information.

What Should We Do

First of all we need to enact stringent laws that should be potent enough to produce deterrent effect. The laws should also shift the burden of proof on the defaulter once *prima facie* the case becomes apparent. Further, these laws need be implemented with equal strictness for everybody. We will have to register cases against known or suspected tax evaders and the corrupt, doing bungling in import export trade, having mafia connections and running drug rackets. For raising the issue with the tax havens or for enlisting the help from the international community, registration of such cases is a pre-requisite.

Second, define tax evasion as criminal offence. Further, the violations of foreign exchange need be brought under the category of crime so that money laundering could be effectively checked and more important the cooperation of other countries could be obtained as they will not be bound to cooperate if these are not defined as criminal offences in our own country.

Third, the treaties have to be concluded again both with the fellow fighting countries as also the countries housing the tax havens. We are yet to start discussion on Double Tax Avoidance treaty with Switzerland though their response was received quite a few months back. Other countries have already signed such treaties with Switzerland and we have also signed with as many as 80 other countries. It is nothing new to us. What surprises is that why it was not done much earlier with Switzerland and the other tax havens when we concluded the same with many other countries. Now, standard formats of all sorts of treaties are available and we should rush through all sided efforts simultaneously instead of causing delays of a few months at every stage.

Fourth, boycott all such tax havens, in political and economic fields, which refuse to cooperate. Like France, close their operations in our country and also our business establishments in their jurisdictions. Basically, India should ban operations by any Indian or foreign firm that has office in any of the tax havens. The tiny islands have grown into giants. If law prohibits our nationals to undertake any business with them or from their soil, they will come down and cooperate. Mauritius falls in such category that has caused much damage to us. We need to come out of their cobweb.

Fifth, establish research cells in government and in the NGO sector to assess, to investigate, to compile and fight for bringing the black money back home as also check its further flight outside. We should seek information not only about the accounts that are current, but also about those that have been closed during last 10 years and obtain all their transactions pertaining to that period as well. If tax havens charge some fee, we should not hesitate to pay that, but get all the details. This information will enable us to identify the people who cheated the nation. Their anti-national deals could be widely exposed and also they should be charged all the taxes alongwith penalties and further penalties should continue to be imposed till such time the money is brought back.

In 2003, when I wrote in the context of the 11th International Anti-corruption Conference, the emphasis was for India creating lobbies to build international pressure on tax havens to get back our money on the model of drug money or the moneys linked to terrorists. At that time it was neither seen nor appreciated as such a big problem on the international screen, though for India it was a very big problem at that time too as in 1996 deposits of Indians in Swiss banks were perceived at $2.55 trillion. The international scenario has since changed drastically. The developed economies after the economic meltdown have already taken a great lead. Now we have only to join and follow them, they are too willing to stand with us and help mutually. We should avail the great opportunity rather fast for not only recovering our moneys, but also for ensuring that there is no siphoning off of our money in future. The process will have to be made very difficult if not impossible.

Following measures are suggested in Indian context in particular, that we could press for adoption. The same holds good for all other countries similarly placed:

(a) Whenever a bank account is opened by an Indian citizen abroad, the particulars of such account should be communicated to the Indian authorities, through its Embassy/High Commission in that country. On receipt, the account number and the other details should be fed into the National Property Register (NPR) immediately and could also be compiled in the CBI. National property registered is visualized as a master computer that will store all the assets in the names of all the individuals with each being allotted a unique identity as per finger print classification or the technologically advanced one proposed to be allotted by the Nilekani Commission.

(b) If a person is found involved in some crime or a criminal case, particularly of corruption, cheating, fraud or any other white-collar crime registered against him in India, then the particulars of balances in account and the copy of the account, if asked for authentically by the investigating agency, should be supplied. One such nodal agency will be nominated by each country. In this context the authorized agency for India could be the CBI. If any state agency or any other agency of the Government of India needs any information, it could approach the CBI. The foreign bank/government should have no option or discretion but to supply duly certified copies of accounts/ information whenever demanded by the nodal agency.

(c) Whenever an Indian purchases a property abroad, its details like those of bank accounts shall be informed by the registering authority there, to the Indian Embassy/High Commission, who will transmit the same to India. This information could also be fed into the National Property Register to be used by the CBI and other agencies as and when required.

(d) Details of all the properties and the bank deposits held abroad by the Indian citizens at present should be supplied to Indian Embassy/High Commission in the respective countries.

(e) Further, on instructions from CBI, the accounts should automatically be frozen, the lockers, the properties and other assets sealed and ultimately these assets be disposed of as per the directions of Indian courts.

(f) For obtaining/supplying such information, the dual criminality may not be insisted upon, as corruption is a crime everywhere, only some technical details may differ. Similarly, the blanket sovereign guarantee of reciprocity may be executed once at the level of the governments and should not be insisted upon for every case separately as that causes tremendous delays.

Once this happens, hiding black incomes abroad will become very difficult and practically impossible. India will start looking up, immediately. But to get such amendments to the rules of the Swiss banks and other tax havens, India has to take pains. This is the most opportune time as the world community is receptive at present.

Even all these efforts are not expected to yield immediate results on their own. The case of USA is different as that mighty country is much cleaner than us, people are more law-abiding, law also is able to strike, their Internal Revenue Service is highly professional and effective, the efforts of government are supported and supplemented by a number of NGO's like GFI that the Swiss had finally to bow to the US and offered to pay a penalty of $780 million and to disclose accounts of 4450 US citizens. Despite all the above, the Swiss withheld information about the remaining 47550 accounts that USA had asked for. Their annual tax loss has been computed at $19 bn. For them it is just a peanut, but they are bothered rather utmost concerned. Somehow we are not bothered though we annually lose much more in absolute terms. We also need to wake up and make persistent efforts.

At the same time India should ratify the UN Convention against Corruption as that will facilitate getting the information as also the funds from tax havens. That would enable us to get the backing of the international community in general and UNO in particular and also establish our goodwill and reputation as a country striving for honesty and integrity. We have already projected ourselves in bad light by not endorsing the treaty during the last six years that shows how the elite have not allowed this step in right direction which enables us to seek cooperation from other countries.

As mentioned above the Nation has been agitated over this issue. This most serious issue was raised by the opposition during the election campaign. Actually, the issue had become relevant in 2001 when in view of 11/9 attack on World Trade Centre in USA the investigators zeroed in on the banking secrecy and found secret bank accounts help facilitate and perpetuate such crimes. Earlier as great Samaritans the Swiss banks had relaxed banking secrecy in case of drug money. After 11/9 the same treatment was extended to terrorism related cases. But the issue claimed the attention the world over after the Interim Revenue Service (IRS) of USA discovered that the Swiss banks operated as tax havens, that they were diverting Amercian money into Swiss banking chain assuring the American citizens of complete secrecy and thereby evading the taxes. The issue had arisen in May 2008 and their inquiries were completed by the end of August, the same year. The US government came down with an iron hand on banking secrecy and threatened the biggest Swiss bank with dire consequences. The issue gathered further momentum in the wake of liquidity crunch with most of the European countries that saw through the significance of this drain on their respective economies. It is in this perspective that all the countries commenced serious efforts against the tax haven the world over. The Swiss government came into picture and agreed for the relaxations mentioned above.

The USA recovered the tax arrears with penalty from its erring citizens but in India nothing such can happen. In all possibility, no inquiries will be allowed; if at all some are ordered, nothing will be made public and ultimately the issues will be diluted without any concrete result in the end. The reason is simple that our elite from all the sections whether bureaucrats, politicians, industrialists, businessmen; all have a stake in protecting the banking secrecy abroad. As such in Indian context it is not easy to take any step in this direction, as the first obstacle is ever present from the Indian elite itself who are holding such accounts/assets abroad. Any government that proposes such steps will face tremendous opposition from inside. Politicians have already taken to slanging match by throwing responsibility on each other and also by arguing that they are not the only bad guys, others such as the powerful bureaucrats, businessmen and industrialists are also equally responsible. They are *prima facie* right that others are also responsible, but then politician is the controller of the system and the final arbiter. The people have entrusted him the responsibility of running the nation and all others work on his behalf and more often for him. Politicians have all the power and prerogative to take action against any erring individual or organization of any denomination. They cannot escape the final accountability. The slanging match is only a ploy and a diversionary tactics. By and large, all of them are sinful in not acting against the black money. They now have to be made to act meaningfully. People should organize pressure groups to compel the government to make all out efforts to seek our money back.

The Tax Havens will not be cowed down easily. They will take protection under various legal provisions and international treaties and decline our request summarily. Even the USA had to exert a lot to the extent of threatening to close down all the 381 branches with 34000 employees of various Swiss banks located in USA, that was one reason that scared the Swiss banks into submission and secondly USA does not suffer from internal contradictions as our government faces here. Our salvation lies in building nationwide pressure on our government.

We can at least immediately close down all the branches of Swiss banks and all other such banks as they shroud themselves in secrecy in India and all these should be barred from entering or doing business with India. Those already functioning be asked to pack off immediately. That will show our seriousness and also lodge an effective protest. Some other developing countries may also follow us, thereby unleashing support for our campaign all over the world. The USA is already leading a campaign against them, but they would go only that far as their national interest demands. We have to take our campaign to the logical end ourselves. But, in view of the changed international scenario and the grounds taken by US, if we take initiative, there would be no problem in the field of international relations or our image in the international community about which we are normally over-concerned. Those existing bankers who want to stay or the new ones who want to enter, should furnish a declaration that there would be no secrecy attached to Indian or foreign operations of Indians and the banks would furnish all the information that may be asked by the Government of India or its chief investigating agency, the CBI by the local branches as also their principals.

In short, still, this will be a long drawn struggle to be based inside and outside the country. It will take decades before our requests are entertained. Even that may happen if intense pressures are exercised on the tax havens by the international community. If India means business, we can join the campaign already underway the world over against the Swiss banks and other tax havens. Further, some of these tax havens belong to big European powers and even the US. When taken up in right earnest still our struggle would be long drawn. To start with, we should break our diplomatic and trade relations with them by casting them out as exploiters of underdeveloped world and conspirators who are receivers of stolen property which is an offence under the Indian Penal Code and the Penal Codes of all the other countries all over the world. This would only mark a beginning that we should intensify and hope to get back our money in part at least, in the coming decades. However the immediate salvation lies in preventing further generation and flight of black money and it is possible very substantially.

The common man is being befooled by all the parties. First, the opposition party contends in election campaign in May 2009 to bring back the Indian black money amounting to $ 1.45 trillion lying in Swiss banks in just 100 days if voted to power. Immediately the party in power reminds them that they were also in power till 2004, why did they not bring it back. The mudslinging, allegations and counter-allegations have been flying in the air as if that brings any relief to the impoverished nation. On the ground we are nowhere near the possibility of getting any relief. After the elections all the heat and mudslinging has disappeared. As usual, once again, there is no mention of black money as if it has ceased to be an issue. Perhaps it will now be dug up near to the 2014 elections to the Union Parliament. On the other hand black money continues to be generated and being drained abroad. Nobody is worried about that. It was very well known that legally it was absolutely impossible to bring back the money except through building pressure on the Swiss authorities and building world opinion that will take decades. Principle of banking secrecy is well enshrined in law and well accepted since ages all over the world and so are the provisions for relaxing the same or cooperating in case the money is linked to crime including corruption. In the field of criminal law certain conditions must be met, otherwise the request will not even be entertained. First of all, it must be crime in both the countries. Second, the treaty arrangements should exist. Third, the requests about individuals alone would be entertained supported by evidence against each that links him to the crime beyond any doubt. Once all this has been done, then only our application would be considered by the courts in that country and not otherwise.

Cases of crime and corruption could be considered, but how many cases of corruption are registered in this country as against the amount drained? Almost negligible. Of these in how many is there evidence to link them to black money abroad? The answer is in the rarest of the rare cases. Manipulation in foreign exchange has ceased to be a criminal offence after FERA was replaced by FEMA. So carting money abroad that is not linked to any substantive crime, by itself is not a criminal offence in India, then how can we even draft an application for getting our money back. But still to befool public our government asked the Swiss bank authorities to give out the names of all those Indians who are keeping secret accounts with them. On 22nd of August we received a big rebuff and Swiss authorities have not only chided us but also upheld the sanctity of the age old secrecy provisions, making us stand in the dock for witch hunting and fishing expeditions. We have made our fight for bringing black money impossible and weaker by weakening the law in India itself. Till such time we strengthen our laws, we should not pin any hope of any help or understanding from the world community. Yet the government applied only to counter the pressure built by the opposition. Both have deliberately befooled the people. However, this befooling game has served a very useful purpose that the people have been educated in the process. They are now more aware and soon will pressurize the government into action.

In the meantime we should concentrate more on internal measures and ensure that black money is not generated any further. An attempt has been made to compile some such measures as outlined in the ensuing chapter.

7

Preventing Generation and Dissemination of Black Money

The analysis in previous chapters has clearly established two issues: First that the black economy thrives on cash transactions as most of the black transactions take place in cash. In order to recover our economy and increase the tax base, cash transactions have to be cut down and so also the cash holdings. A large number of business houses, politicians and corrupt government servants stash tens and hundreds of crores of rupees even in gunny bags in some dingy dark corners of their houses about which stories are heard from time to time either in social gatherings or when sometimes the income tax department or the CBI unearths such holdings in their raids. Second, it is the generation of black money that is crucial from our angle as the accumulations abroad are beyond our control at least in the short run.

If the cash transactions could be restricted to the minimum necessary, the recorded economy will grow and that will reduce or eliminate creation of black money and augment the amount collected as taxes. The phenomenon of black money can directly be correlated to the currency in circulation in our country that is just burgeoning. Not only its ratio to GDP is very high as compared to other countries, but its rate of growth is also much higher in comparison. At present the cash to GDP ratio of India is 14.45 percent as compared to 5.9 percent of USA. The table 7.1 below gives comparison between different countries for 2003 for which period comparative figures are available.

Table 7.1: Cash to GDP ratio for

Advanced Economies-2003		Asian Economies-2004	
Canada	3.7 percent	South Korea	2.5 percent
France	3.6 percent	Taiwan	6.6 percent
Germany	6.2 percent	Malaysia	6.4 percent
Italy	5.8 percent	Hong Kong	10.9 percent
Japan	14.4 percent	Singapore	7.6 percent
U K	3.7 percent	Indonesia	4.7 percent
USA	6.0 percent	Thailand	9.3 percent
Euro area	5.6 percent	Philippines	5.4 percent
India	12.27 percent	India	12.6 percent

The ratio has rather diminished Sharply during last 4-5 years in other countries that are comparatively clean. It has declined there by 2-3 percent of the GDP whereas in India it has mounted up by similar percentage from 12.6 to 14.45 in 2008.

Currencies like Dollar, Pound sterling, Euro and even Yen of Japan play the role of global medium of exchang; Hong Kong and Singapore also nurture global markets. Naturally these currencies are in demand beyond the local requirements whereas Indian currency is for local use only, but still not only our ratio is higher but is also on sharp rise.

The reasons are not far to seek. In these countries most of the transactions take place through the bank money i.e. cheques, bank drafts or the plastic money. That obviates the need for cash. In India, on the other hand, most of the transactions take place in cash and also there is heavy demand for storage purposes coming from the highest strata of the society. First, having proved this hypothesis, we have to analyse and locate the causes of the problem, its mechanics, the consequential problems that are generated and finally the solutions. The lower sections of the society have very limited income and so is also the size of their transactions that are small and a few. The following data on household consumption giving statistics about the monthly personal consumption expenditure was quoted by the Finance Minister in the context of the improvement in the position of people below the poverty line in the Economic Survey 2008-09 that preceded the presentation of the budget. The data is very meaningful and clearly brings home the point. (See Table 7.2)

As per the Survey conducted by the CSO (Central Statistical Organisation) the figure of people below poverty line for the year 2004-05 was 27.5 percent by Uniform Recall Period (URP) Method. Finding it too high, the Government changed the criterion to Monthly Per Capita Expenditure (MPCE) for the household. The CSO on the basis of new criterion conducted the fresh survey in 2007 called the National Sample Survey Report No. 527 on Household Consumer Expenditure in India. The report covered three years from 2004-05 to 2006-07. The population percentage below the poverty line for 2004-05 dropped by 6 points to 21.6 percent. The instant analysis is based on this very report. In Table 7.2, the first two columns have been taken from that report for 2006-07 as reproduced in the Economic Survey 2008-09. It shows the most favourable position, but even this is alarming. It is in two parts for rural and urban areas, column 1 depicts the monthly expenditure of the household, column 2, the total percentage of population falling below each income level. Column 3 has been deduced by subtracting previous level of population from the subsequent level to give the net population percentage at the particular

Table 7.2: Monthly Personal Consumption Expenditure

MPCE level 2006-07 percent of population below the level at current prices	Population %age below the indicated level	Population %age at the indicated level	Population at the indicated level (in crores)	Total monthly consumption expenditure (in crores of rupees)
Total pop 112 crores				
Rural 78 crores Urban 34 crores				
1	2	3	4	5
		RURAL		
235	1.2	1.20	0.9	219.96
270	3.2	2.00	1.6	421.20
320	7.5	4.30	3.4	1,073.28
365	12.7	5.20	4.1	1,480.44
410	20.8	8.10	6.3	2,590.38
455	29.1	8.30	6.5	2,945.67
510	39.0	9.90	7.7	3,938.22
580	50.3	11.30	8.8	5,112.12
690	64.9	14.60	11.4	7,857.72
890	80.3	15.40	12.0	10,690.68
1155	90.6	10.30	8.0	9,279.27
Rural Total (Monthly)				45,608.94
		URBAN		
335	1.5	1.50	0.5	170.85
395	3.9	2.40	0.8	322.32
485	9.5	5.60	1.9	923.44
580	17.4	7.90	2.7	1,557.88
675	25.8	8.40	2.9	1,927.80
790	35.0	9.20	3.1	2,471.12
930	46.1	11.10	3.8	3,509.82

Contd...

1	2	3	4	5
1100	57.2	11.10	3.8	4,151.40
1380	70.3	13.10	4.5	6,146.52
1880	82.9	12.60	4.3	8,053.92
2540	91.4	8.50	2.9	7,340.60
Urban Total (monthly)				**36,575.67**
Rural Total (monthly)				**45,608.94**
GRAND TOTAL (ANNUAL)				**9,86,215.32**

level of expenditure. Column 4 gives out the actual number of people in a particular level out of the total rural/urban population, based on the percentage in column 3. Lastly column 5 records the total expenditure by the chunk of population falling in a particular expenditure group i.e. by multiplying expenditure level in column 1 with actual population at that level as worked out in column 4. As per census projections, the population of the country has been taken as 112 crores with rural population at 70 percent and urban population at 30 percent working out to 78 crores and 34 crores respectively for the year 2007.

The total expenditure of 91 percent households, both rural and urban, amounts to 9.86 lac crores for 2007, or only 23.8 percent of the recorded GDP of 41.29 lac crores, whereas the remaining 76.2 percent of the GDP is cornered by just the 9 percent. Incidentally entire black money/income is also the preserve of this 9 percent of population. With parallel economy of equal size, this upper section gets 76.2 +100=176.2 out of the total national cake of 200. Their percentage share in reality thus works out to 88 whereas 91 percent of people share only the remaining 12. This 91 percent section lives from hand to mouth, under perpetual debt and their propensity to save is zero. It is no secret that thousands of them commit suicide every year as they find it difficult to survive. Whatever money they get, is spent the same day immediately i.e. their money moves very fast or in other words the velocity of money with them is very high i.e. 365. In reality it is much higher than 365 even, in the sense that if they get money for the month at the month end and they spend the entire amount the same day instead of spending on pro-rata basis during the next 30 days. As such, the velocity of money with them should be reckoned 30 times higher. However, even if we peg that at a low of 200, the cash required for all their transactions would be the quotient of their total expenditure divided by 200 which works out to Rs. 4,928 crores at the most or say five thousand crores only.

There are reasons that the requirement of cash is lower still by this section of population. A large number of cultivators grow their own food and most of their other requirements. Their dependence on cash as such is very limited. Further, a large sector in rural India still practices barter to a considerable extent. In the whole of the country excepting the states of Punjab, Haryana, Maharashtra and Tamilnadu, the agricultural labour is only partly paid in cash, though in states like Bihar, almost the entire payment is still in kind. The standard wage rates there since ages have been 4-5 kg rice/paddy per day. The rate has by and large remained unaffected by the developments around; leading to continuous struggle for raising it to at least 6 kg, but the success has eluded. Even when raised to that level, still it will be much below the prescribed minimum wages. Irrespective of the concepts of economic or the social justice, the fact is that the requirement of cash in the circumstances remains very low and further they do not need the higher denomination notes at all. Even if they were to conduct all their transactions in cash, in view of their small income, their requirement of cash will be highly limited. Under these circumstances 91 percent of the population does not deal with or require 500 or 1000 rupee denomination notes and perhaps in a very limited way with 100 rupee notes. For them 10, 20 and at the most 50 rupee notes are more than sufficient.

Coming to the requirement of cash for the remaining income of Rs. 31.43 lac crores; first, let us account for the savings. Savings in our economy are to the extent of 23 percent or Rs. 9.5 lac crores. Some minimum levels of transactions say 10 to 20 percent do take place through banks as well. Let us account for all these including savings at just 20 percent of the GDP working out to Rs. 8.25 lac crores on all these counts. At best the business left to be transacted by cash is only Rs. 23.18 lac crores. Even if we presume that a particular note on an average is used only once in two weeks, the velocity of money comes to 26 in a year. No data about the velocity of money is available, so it has to be analysed and presumed only. Thus the cash required to conduct transactions worth Rs. 23.18 lac crores would amount to Rs. 89154 crores only. Adding the requirement of lower sections, as worked out earlier, the total amounts to Rs. 94154 crores only. The remaining amount of over Rs. 6 lac crores is needed to store and to conduct black transactions. Part of it goes into the dead storage and a part moves the wheels of the other (black) economy. Thus out of the Rs. 7.20 lac crores of currency as on 3 June 2009 as per Reserve Bank of India Weekly statistics, Rs. 7.15 lac crores is the requirement of 9 percent population. Though basically this section should transact business through banking channels as this is all educated gentry having access to banking system and credit/debit cards, but this very section steeped deeply in the black money transactions, requires more and more notes for purposes of storage. Since storage is fraught with greater risk if volume of the cash is larger, so the notes of higher denominations are preferred. It is for this reason that the demand for higher denomination notes is on the rise progressively. Not only the 100 rupee note is out of favour, but the demand for even 500 rupee note is on the decline as compared to 1000 rupee note. Demand for 1000 rupee note is soaring steeply despite the risk of higher probability of counterfeiting.

The above analysis leads directly to two conclusions. First, most of the Indian population has very limited requirement for cash for the reasons that the volume of all their transactions that their economic power allows are highly limited, if not insigificant. Second, the overwhelming proportion of them receives cash and spends it immediately in its entirety. With high velocity of money with them, even a small amount of cash is enough to perform all their transactions. Their demand for storage is nil. That proves the hypothesis that high demand for cash is for transactions in black as also for storing the trash that cannot be kept with banks. Though in all fairness the use of cash by higher echelons of society should be rather exception and its volume highly restricted. They should be spending through the bank money or the plastic money that in any case is so convenient. In my family not more than 20 percent of transactions are conducted in cash that too for the reason that a number of shopkeepers do not accept credit cards as they transact their business in black and they want to hide their black income. No wonder, as described in the earlier chapter, that the businessman in question spent Rs. 3 lacs per month in the joint family, but declared an income of only Rs. 10000 per month. As high as 97 percent of his household transactions are in black and hence have to be in cash. Besides his household expenditure, he requires more currency for running his business as also for storing the slush. If our countrymen did not indulge in black money, perhaps all the bonafide transactions could be performed with cash just about two percent of the GDP that corresponds to Rs. 90,000 crores for 2006-07. Perhaps the remaining cash equivalent to 12 percent of the GDP is for the black market, black transactions and for storing the black money.

The Table 7.3 very clearly shows that the demand for 100 rupee notes has stagnated over the years, but the same is on rise for 500 and 1000 rupee notes and the rate of increase is the highest in case of 1000 rupee notes. This is the disturbing scenario indicating the extent of black market operations. If others viz Americans, European or even Asian countries can transact their business with an amount of currency between 2 to 5 percent of their GDP, why should we in India need as high an amount as 14.45 percent that too when income distribution in our economy is so poised that 91 percent need very little and the rest, to be fair, should need still less. Unfortunately, it is these low income people in the name of whose illiteracy and ignorance the arguments for not making use of banking instruments mandatory, are coined. It appears. that out of the four functions of money namely a Standard, Measure, Medium and a Store that the school text books on Economics prescribe, it is primarily the storage function that is the most predominant out of the two operative functions of medium and store, whereas the money was basically designed as medium of exchange but it is being misused mainly as a store by the elite.

Two major issues along with attendant offshoots emerge having direct bearing on the problem. First, that not only the Cash GDP ratio is very high, but the number of higher denomination notes is also very high and further the demand for them is growing very fast and the rate of growth of this demand itself is on the rise. The Table 7.3 from the Annual Reports of RBI on Currency Management, shows the annual overall increase in the currency, the share of higher denomination notes as also the high rate of growth.

Table 7.3: Currency in Circulation Denomination-wise

(Value in crores of Rs.)

Year End March				Total currency (including 2 to 50 Rupee notes)
Denomination of notes	100	500	1000	
2001	1,08,141	52,947	3,719	2,12,460
2002	1,18,041	68,512	7,179	2,44,713
2003	1,15,386	93,813	15,971	2,75,096
2004	1,21,442	1,22,938	27,473	3,19,761
2005	1,23,282	1,52,728	42,082	3,61,229
2006	1,34,640	1,82,350	64,300	4,21,911
2007	1,35,444	2,25,400	93,676	4,96,138
2008	1,34,575	2,63,108	1,41,219	5,81,598
2009	1,37,028	3,08,304	1,91,784	6,81,113
June 2009				7,20,521

It is self-explanatory that the rate of increase in the currency and in particular that of higher denomination notes is far beyond the recorded rate of growth of the economy. For the last few years the supply of currency has grown @ 15 to 17 percent, but the supply of higher denomination notes has grown by 25 percent for 500 rupee notes and by 50 percent in case of 1000 rupee notes, incredible. Only in 2008-09, when growth is around 6 percent, the rate of increase of supply of the two denominations of notes has come down but is still 17 and 36 percent respectively. Absolute increase is as high as Rs. 99515 crores of which 95700 crores is for the two highest denominations. With economic growth averaging at about 6 percent, the excess supply of money causes inflation. If it represents deficit financing, it is a very dangerous matter if it is not accompanied by corresponding growth. Deficit financing without growth only transfers economic power from the poorer sections of the society to the higher sections and disproportionate demand for notes of higher denomination confirms and points to further growth of black money in the economy.

But even in case of deficit financing, money in the form of currency needs not be thrown in the market. Money be pumped through the banking channels, so that it does not get lost in the black money stream and reaches the correct hands through the productive streams breaking the mafia channels as Rajiv Gandhi had regretted, but till this day no one has taken any fruitful steps to control that.

Second major and very significant issue is that during the meltdown, the income levels are supposed to have gone down, so should also be the transactions in the market. But the demand for currency has not shown any such trend. The demand has been continuously rising. The only possible reason that comes to mind is that in view of the depression, the black money is being withdrawn from the speculative activities that are being temporarily suspended. There is as such more of unaccounted liquidity to be stored, necessitating the need for more cash and that too for the higher denomination notes.

Clearly, there is need to encourage the use of plastic money and to make payments through the banking instruments. Cheques, however, have a limitation that these cannot be accepted from the strangers in the general market and also a number of fraud cases arise out of them. From this angle, till a few years back cash was irreplaceable, but now plastic money is as good as cash rather better, in the sense that carrying cash is hazardous but not the credit or debit card, which in any case is the perfect substitute of the cash. A time has come when use of cash be forbidden by law to defray any transaction of and beyond Rs. 1000.This size of transaction can be performed by 10 notes of 100 rupee or 20 and 50 notes of 50 and 20 rupee denomination. 91 percent of population seldom performs transactions bigger than that. Of the remaining nine percent also half of them have limited access to black money and do not have very large personal economies, for whom 100 rupee note will be adequate. It is basically a problem created and perpetuated by a mere four percent or still lower proportion of the population. However even their absolute number is four crores, equivalent to some of the bigger countries of the world as there are only 27 countries in the world that have population more than 4 crores. In themselves this upper crust constitutes separate couple of financial nationalities; some amongst them super high and the others only high; depending upon their financial status and connections abroad. Except exploiting the country internally for their lawful and more often unlawful pursuits they have nothing to do with the nation. They are expected to use plastic money or the banking channels so that their incomes get accounted and they pay income tax and the other due taxes. But the problem is precisely with this section as they only indulge in the black transactions that per force have to be in cash. Those who do not indulge in black, do not require cash even for a transaction of 1000 as they will use credit/debit card beyond a couple of hundred of rupees.

If the notes of rupees 500 and 1000 denomination are withdrawn (through a regulated mechanism) as legal tender, the transactions per force will take place through credit card/debit card/cheques/bank drafts; the recording of economy will improve. Now the banks have reached every nook and corner of the country, so it has become possible to enforce the use of bank money. It has been amply demonstrated that the lower sections of society i.e. at least 91 percent of the population does not feel the need for even the 100 rupee note what to say of 500 rupee note. Higher denomination is not the requirement of the masses and they will not be affected if these notes are demonetized. On the other hand the higher sections should not be allowed the use of cash as they are capable of using bank money and also their transactions are of heavy value.

However, at the same time it has to be ensured that such withdrawal does not inflict undue misery on any genuine holder of higher denomination notes whichever class he may belong to. Such persons will have to be protected. It is proposed to prescribe a specific regulatory mechanism that will ensure that it will not be blindfold demonitisation, but only a systematic withdrawal of notes in the process of exchange of value for the honest citizens and an exposing device for those indulging in black money. With this end in view, upto 2 notes of Rs. 1000 or 4 notes of Rs. 500 denomination or a mix of the two upto the value of Rs. 2000 shall be entertained for direct conversion into 100 rupee or the smaller denomination notes, for any individual within four weeks of the notification. To ensure that the same person does not repeat the process the indelible ink mark shall be put on his finger just like at the time of voting. All the higher denomination notes presented by any individual beyond the total value of Rs. 2000 shall be credited into his specially opened bank account if presented within four weeks of the notification to this effect and the account will be treated as frozen automatically. After four weeks time the higher denomination notes will cease to be legal tender and will not be entertained either for encashment or for being deposited. Some people, who cannot explain the legitimacy of money, may choose not to deposit the money at all. This money will automatically lapse to the state as the notes after the due date will be rendered useless pieces of paper. Those who can show that their money is properly accounted will be allowed to operate their accounts through bank money only with some small regulated drawal of cash in smaller denomination notes for which the detailed rules will have to be framed. If one deposits money in a bank, he will have to prove within 30 days his title to the money and he gets it back, or declares within 30 days that he cannot prove its legitimacy and surrenders himself to the clemency of the government, a flat charge of 40 percent of income tax shall be deducted and he will be allowed to operate the remaining 60 percent. If he chooses not to surrender and at the same time cannot prove his title to the money within 30 days, income tax at the rate of 50 percent shall be recovered immediately and the remaining money be frozen for a period of three months in which period he will have to prove that the money was not unaccounted. If he cannot prove, the entire amount shall lapse to the state.

India will not be the first country to demonetize higher denomination notes, some other countries have done it before. USA in 1969 and Malaysia in 1990 are the ready recent examples that demonetized the higher currency. South Korea demonetized higher currency in 2006 mainly for checking the onslaught of counterfeit notes. Moreover most of the countries do not have currency representing more than 100 units. USA, Australia, Malaysia, all have highest notes of only 100 dollars or ringgits, whereas in UK the highest note is of 50 pound sterling only. If Switzerland has 1000 franc currency notes, their position as repository of black wealth from all over the world, is understandable as they have to enable people to carry their cash in easy packages. It may be argued that our rupee represents too small a value. *Prima facie* there appears to be some substance, no doubt, but a little insight will show that as a unit of purchasing power, the rupee is not so small when viewed in context of small incomes and the prevailing price levels in this country. It is well known and follows from the table 7.2 that half of Indian population lives on less than half a dollar per head per day as against $136 in USA. With incomes at such a low level, what these people are going to do with higher denomination notes? These are required by and meant for higher echelons of society say top 4-5 percent and help them conceal their black money and also help in conducting the black transactions. The Government, I am sure, should not propose to be a facilitator or an abettor to their nefarious designs. There is no justification for retaining higher denomination notes.

Discontinuation of higher denomination notes will bestow many other direct and indirect advantages besides solving the problem of black money to a very large extent. First of all, the transactions in the economy will come under control. The size of unaccounted economy will shrink and that of the accounted economy will grow up and that too very fast, adding ultimately an equal economy of Rs. 51 lac crores to the existing economy of that measure for the year 2008-09.

Second, the foremost effect will be that with reining in of black money, the tax collections will not only look up, but soar very high. The recorded income, as we have seen, will rise to double i.e. over Rs. 100 lac crores a year and tax compliance will also automatically rise matching with the world averages. Against the OECD average of 36 percent of GDP as taxes, even if we are able to reach a 30 percent level, we would collect a whopping sum of Rs. 30 lac crores as taxes against the present level of Rs. 8.54 lac crores in 2007-08 as per Economic Survey. With this magnitude of economic power in the hands of the governments (both central and states), this can do wonders. The governments will be able to meet effectively with the requirements of all the sectors say economic, infrastructure, defence, education, social services etc. The blackmailing by various contracting firms, industries and foreign governments will cease as we will not beseech them with a begging bowl. We have seen in the previous chapters how on an investment of 700 crores, the country is being bled to the extent of 24000 crores and still the blackmail is going on as it is obvious from the first statement of minister Kamal Nath after taking over the ministry that even these exorbitant rates have fallen short and the firms want still higher rates for taking up works under BOT.

Third, there could not be a better instance of the misuse of higher denomination notes for facilitating the storage, the transport and conducting big transactions than the recent case of Madhu Koda. As per media reports he deposited Rs. 640 crores in cash in a branch of the Union Bank of India at Mumbai. It seems improbable but has not been contradicted by the bank. The only reaction in the Press has been a statement of the spokesman of the bank that they did not commit any irregularity.

Legality or culpability apart, it is as good as a confirmation that this huge amount was credited in cash into the bank. He could move as large a consignment worth Rs. 640 crores only because of big denomination notes. But for these notes, he would have to move a number of trucks giving out secrecy without which such clandestine movement is not possible. Without such notes, the big transactions in cash would become difficult if not impossible. With 500 and 1000 rupee notes gone, even if 100 rupee notes are managed to be collected for a big amount, it will constitute 5 to 10 times the volume and weight in comparison to present when big notes are available. Carrying cash in 100 rupee notes will pose a big problem as allegedly faced by Harshad Mehta for carrying just one crore that he is alleged to have taken to the residence of the then Prime Minister PV Narsimha Rao in early 90s.He had generated a big controversy and embarrassment for himself and the PM as well. Transaction of land and houses these days run into tens and hundreds of crores that may require a whole truck if payment is to be made in 100 rupee notes, exposing to the danger of being looted. Smaller notes by themselves act as deterrent in big transactions and bring more of economy into the domain of accounting.

Fourth, the problem of counterfeit currency will be contained. Many countries resorted to this step to tackle this problem. Pakistan and Bangladesh are both hard set to destroy our economy by flooding it with counterfeit currency. With every passing year the capture of counterfeit currency detected by banks and apprehended by police and CBI is on steep rise. Recently a team of Mumbai police investigating the source of the counterfeit notes of Rs. 1,000 denomination that were seized, believe that the fake notes were printed in a "government press" belonging to a neighbouring country. The frequency of apprehension of gangs of fake currency has been on rise and there operations are also growing in size. In July 2009, six people were caught supplying fake 1,000 rupee denomination notes amounting to about Rs. 4 lac in Mumbai. This was followed by a series of similar arrests in Hyderabad, Goa and Bangalore. A gang apprehended in Madhya Pradesh in June 2009 made startling disclosures that they were assigned to the state of MP. In the last six months, they exchanged around Rs. 10 lac worth currency in four districts that were placed under their charge for the purpose. In all the places the gang members ostensibly supplied some unskilled labour from Malda, a town in West Bengal. The gang had sent four such parties in Central India as per his knowledge. The gang leader also disclosed that the factories manufacturing such notes were running in Bangladesh and on Indian side it was a flourishing trade. It is also a matter of fact that a very small percentage of such counterfeit currency that is in circulation, can be apprehended as the quality of these fake notes is very high that the ordinary people find it difficult to decipher. These have been printed on the authentic imported paper. The culprits have emulated with fineness and accuracy the new security features introduced by the Indian authorities that make it difficult to distinguish. Producing such high-quality notes requires involvement of government apparatus and knowhow including the services of the printing press that our neighbours are too eager to extend to criminals at the level of the government. Such fake currency is also ploughed in funding terrorism. By demonetizing, we will be saving our economy, from enemies both external and internal and would also be cutting the lifeline of the terrorists by depriving them of ready finances.

Fifth, it will cut down the cost of supply of currency notes as the requirement of notes will steeply decline as the security paper is entirely an imported item. This step will mean a lot of savings to the nation.

Sixth, the crime of kidnapping for ransom, dacoity, robbery and housebreaking particularly by domestic servants will fall, since black money cannot be kept in banks, the cash or jewellery is stashed in the safe confines of one's house. That may be hidden from the view of the outside world but nothing is hidden from the valet as the proverb goes. This attracts him. Besides, he also knows that this money has been cornered through underhand means or in other words is born out of crimes/frauds/tax evasion of various descriptions. So; he feels no compunction of the soul and loots the unaccounted cash and jewellery, just as his master did, without any sense of guilt. Further looting cash from such businesses like petrol pumps that at present collect heavy cash because of the predominant cash transactions and carry it for being deposited in the bank or kept in the safe environs of household, will become redundant as sales by plastic money will obviate all that. So the crime of loot and the accompanying murder will automatically decline.

Seventh, the dowry problem will also ease to a large extent. I see dowry as a function of black money economy. At the highest economic ladder, it is happy exchange of gifts and a mechanism for laundering the slush by the elite as their money gets converted from black to white. It is well known that in our country, everything related to marriage is treated as sacrosanct and even the tax sleuths seldom question the items received in marriage. Though, by itself the word dowry may be abominable, but there is nothing wrong with whatever is received in marriage. Incidentally the Central Government has imposed a gift tax @30 percent, but gifts in marriage that are nothing but dowry, have been excluded altogether, irrespective of their value. Once the incomes are recorded, no one will be so eager to part with their hard earned resources. That apart, as per the system visualized in this work, cash transactions will cease to be there. All transaction will be recorded and known. The need to use the occasion of marriage for conversion will cease to exist.

Last, but not the least, the lower sections of society will get paid fully in an accounted economy, and further the governments equipped with larger resources will be able to look after the welfare of all and in particular the lower sections of society, who will be able to find gainful employment that will by itself prevent youth from taking to Naxalism and such like other activities.

National Property Register

There is need to record all the assets, movable as also immovable, held by any Indian in India or abroad, in a way that the position in totality appears on the screen in one go. Cash, gold and the real estate are the most popular repositories of black money kept within the country. Transactions in black economy are conducted in cash, but it may not be possible to have any check on cash holdings except through periodic raids. However, real estate transactions are all recorded, though there are lots of frauds committed and cheating of the exchequer in the process. As examined in details earlier, the registration authority plays a significant role in this loot. The bunglings at registration office are manifold. Besides depressing the rates of the property for purposes of registration, the identities of sellers and purchasers are not ascertained and are often allowed to be confused deliberately so that the owner cannot be traced or identified; the transactions turn 'Benami'. Further, it is well known that whenever government sells/allots any houses for economically weaker sections, the land sharks purchase these in the name of the poor people by paying them some pittance and after the mandatory minimum period, get it transferred in their own names. A few years later palatial buildings come up on the site. This is what happened to Madangir, originally allotted as a Jhuggi Jhonpri colony in South Delhi, now boasts of a palatial marketing centre. The shark decentralizes his properties that too in different names, ensuring that detection and accounting are almost impossible. The crucial point that emerges is to bring all these assets at one place under a unique identity number.

Till a few years back, it was unthinkable to compile and compute such properties of an individual, but now with advancements in computers it has easily become possible. Computers of almost unlimited storage and processing capacity are available. Data regarding all registrations all over the country can be stored, processed and retrieved as per requirement. With suitable software it is possible to process the entire range of data in the desired manner. The system can function as detailed below.

All property transactions and other transactions/acquisitions relating to assets should be entered at *tehsil* and district level computers. These district level computers should be linked to the state level computer, which could retrieve information from district computer directly. The network could similarly extend to the national level computer chain, managed by NICNET. These days all the state governments have connected the state headquarters with districts, sub-divisions and tehsils, so retrieval of information over this network is possible at every level. This computer network is visualised as the National Property Register. Income tax department could also access it, and also feed data into it or retrieve from it.

The registering authority should obtain legible and decipherable fingerprints along with photographs of the purchaser as also of the seller. The prints should be classified generating a separate file for each such individual and then only the registration deed should be executed. All properties in the name of this particular person will get collected in the computer at one place in this file generated on the basis of his fingerprint classification. The photograph of the purchaser should become part and parcel of the file. In his file, a reference can be made to all such other files of his family members, so that all the family properties can be located immediately. Besides property, the details of all their bank accounts could also be stored in this register. For the purpose, the bank should obtain and forward the finger prints to the NPR (National Property Register) where these will be classified and fed into the computer and integrated to the property transactions. With a single identification system to be evolved by the Nilekani Commission, the job will become simpler still. At the time of investigation of a disproportionate assets case, search can be mounted on the national hook-up all over the country. The accused cannot then hide the properties and other assets in his name or in the name of any other member of his family. For purposes of conducting search, the law should provide that in investigations of a registered criminal case under Prevention of Corruption Act, the family members of an accused should be obliged to give their fingerprints. This will enable the IO to trace all the family assets. Further, only the person whose fingerprint identification is on record should be allowed to make a sale. All the payments will be made by the bank draft which will get added to the page of the seller. That may reduce dependence on Benami as this person has to account for and receive all the payments through cheque or bank draft. Transfer back to the real owner, in case of 'Benami' transactions may pose problems and discourage the people from indulging in such activities. The computer will be able to link an individual to the property and vice versa. If a property cannot be linked to the person in whose name it is registered, it should lapse to the state. Introduction of national property register may curb speculative purchases of real estate and release lots of properties from the clutches of the sharks. It may also arrest the prohibitive property prices, particularly in urban areas that pose a grave threat to the stability of the economy.

Register Marriage Places and Regulate Them

Marriage industry has emerged as the biggest game of black money. An attempt has been made to demonstrate how costly the marriages are and use, by and large, all the black money as all the taxes are evaded and the black money from unrecorded sector plays a very vital role. Besides, the demonitisation of higher currency will have a great bearing on this industry. In order to regulate this industry, the first step is to register the marriage places and a minimum charge including all the fees and taxes due to the government, be made mandatory to be deposited in government treasury before any celebrations can take place. The entire celebrations should be videotaped by the income tax department. The amount of advance should be determined on the basis of minimum prescribed number of guests and a return of the actual expenditure incurred should be filed within 30 days after the marriage and more amount if due should be credited to the treasury. The videotaping would help determine the actual expenditure. However, there can be no question of any refund out of the advance as that being the minimum.

Limit on Cash Transactions

Transactions in cash require being limited to very basics say upto just one thousand rupees beyond which the plastic money or the banking channels should be used. As has been seen at length in earlier chapters the cash transactions that leave no trail behind are the biggest culprit in generating and sustaining the black economy that requires to be controlled.

Realistic Tax Rates

The tax rates should be realistic as unnecessary low rates deprive the exchequer of the resources reducing thereby the capacity of the government to provide the expected services. On the other hand very high tax rates lead to total evasion as gains of evasion rise proportionately higher and the risk becomes more and more worth taking. To an honest citizen paying VAT at 12.5 percent, that too on necessities of life, pinches too hard and it saps his economic power, whereas, for a person dishonest from the point of view of payment of tax, the higher the rate the greater the gain and so is also the incentive for evading it. One wonders if our tax system is serving the people and the exchequer or only the tax evader. In Haryana the VAT on building material is 12.5 percent, but only 10 percent of the sales come on record. Consequently the effective rate of tax falls to 1.25 percent. On catering particularly in marriage banquets (leaving out the 5 star hotels) the billing is to the tune of 5 percent only. The tax of 12.5 percent is meaningless as the recovery is hardly 0.6 percent. On registry the rate of fee may be 6 to 8 percent of the consideration, but as we saw the market rates of plots are 16 times as compared to the circle rates; so the actual recovery is only 0.375 to 0.5 percent of the due. On the other hand, the tax rates on some luxury items are abysmally low. On jewellery, the rate is 1 to 2 percent in various states. Beyond any dispute it is a luxury item and the money involved is also very substantial. The fear that high rate of VAT will give a Philip to smuggling, is inconsequential. Laws are not abandoned for fear of non-implementation. Taking this argument further the best way to get rid of the crime is that do not define any aberration as crime and the society will be crime free. This is what the police forces do all over the country that they do not register crime and then shout from rooftop that crime is on decline. UP has consistently done so and has achieved incredible results. The IPC crime in the state has fallen from 2.40 lac in 1970 to just 1.02 lac 35 years later, though the population has gone up by 250% and all the other factors leading to crime have gone up. Nithari tragedy was the direct fall out of this very cheating enforced on the society. Whether it is the field of crime control or tax collection, the principle is equally true. In all such cases, the need is not to deny or suppress the problem, but to strengthen the enforcement. Finance minister should refrain from leading the nation that way. This industry has a minimum market share of Rs. five lac crores in black and may extend up to eight lac crores. No finance minister can afford to ignore such a big chunk of the economy that too in the sphere of luxury. One gets the impression that since it largely caters to the elitist sections of the society, it is another perk that they have arrogated or misappropriated at the cost of the exchequer.

The concept should be that the rates be reasonable as warranted solely by economic considerations, neither too low nor too high.

But in any case the luxury items should be taxed higher. Whereas, on the ground the ordinary building material is subject to a tax rate of 10 to 12 percent and a top luxury item like jewellery bears only a token tax. What a violation of the basics in a welfare state. In case of jewellery people are serious to get bill for the reason that they require receipt, may be Benami, to get an assurance about the purity. The belief gets re-enforced that the low tax rate is only to facilitate the elite or a vote catching device as all women have weakness for gold, jewellery etc and it is a mechanism to target them as against the national, social and the economic interests of the country.

As the economy comes more and more under record, apart from the collection of indirect taxes, more important is that the income tax will have to be paid on accounted incomes that would be @ 30 percent. With rational indirect taxes, when most of the customers will start asking for the bill, that would be the beginning of the purge.

Make All Government Payments Through Banks

As discussed earlier, everyone who matters, realizes and agrees with the latest observation of Rahul Gandhi that only 10 percent of the intended money reaches the correct person particularly in rural areas. Further, where the labour in rural areas is paid in kind, it is at half the rates as in Bihar 5 kg of course rice will mean Rs. 40 only. All the payments in rural areas and in particular on account of the government be channelized into the bank accounts of the labour. If necessary the accounts may specially be opened with the banks. It will be desirable that the private sector including the building industry that employs people on day to day basis be paid through banks. This will also bring their economic activities on record. That will ensure that the remaining 90 percent or Rs. 1.26 lac crores also reaches the person to whom it belongs. Let us not take pity on him as a poor person, only ensure that what he has earned reaches him. He needs Justice and Not Pity.

Liberate Auditors from Companies /Individuals

Independent audit is another measure at cleansing that was stonewalled. Before the bursting of Enron, it was not taken seriously in the United States also, though it had assumed mafia like proportions about which warnings had come decades earlier from prominent personalities. Theodore Roosevelt, the then US President (in 1901-10) referring to the role of auditing had observed, "Behind the ostensible government sits enthroned an invisible government owing no allegiance and acknowledging no responsibility to the people. To destroy this invisible governance to defoil the unholy alliance between corrupt business and corrupt politics is the first task of the statesmanship of the day." How prophetic the words were, spoken almost a century ago. The US ignored and it had to pay with many scams culminating finally in the Enron scandal that shook not only the US but the whole world that is now trying to fight out both Frauds and Corruption through various means and organizations not only inside the country but also in international arena. The efforts of OECD countries in curbing bribery in international trade are appreciable. The 2006 TI (Transparency International) report on OECD countries, amongst others, has recommended promoting Corporate Compliance Programme and raising accounting and auditing requirements and standards.

The audit in private sector has been a farce everywhere. In the words of George Bush it has been mired in the mindset of "cooking the books, shading the truth, and breaking our laws" that the President vowed to "do everything in our power to end the same .....as.... In the long run there is no capitalism without conscience..." After all the world over including the USA and Europe, the firms that saw biggest scams were supervised by the biggest firms of Accountants and Auditors. A few major scams the world saw in recent past are as follows:

USA	Europe
Enron	Ahold (Dutch)
WorldCom	Parmalat (Italy)
Global Crossing	Vivendi Universal (France)
Health South	Leonart and Hauspie (Belgium)
Hollinger (Canada)	Satyam (India)

Despite the fact that all had employed reputed Auditors out of:

Arthur Anderson

Ernest and Young

Price Waterhouse Cooper

Grant Thourton

Deloitte

Touche

It is obvious that thorough examination was lacking and certain persons had some motives that were not honourable. To contain this menace of "high-profile business failures, such as Enron and WorldCom and in order to reform public company accounting and to reinforce investor`s confidence", US immediately enacted Sarbanes-*Oxley (SOX) Act of 2002* .One finds it difficult to digest why they did not enact the relevant laws earlier as even otherwise great emphasis has existed in US on probity in public life as George Washington, the first President, prescribed ethics in public service as early as 1789 that we have failed to prescribe till this day. The same were amended by the 'Ethics in Government Act, 1978', further strengthened by the Principles of Ethical Conduct for Government Officers and Employees 1989. Corresponding provisions continued to be extended in private sector as well. Singapore did very well by enacting similar laws right from 1959 after winning independence that very year.

How true are the observations of Roosevelt in our context even today after a full century! Basic reason why Audit takes that irresponsible attitude appears to be that the firm or the individual himself employs the Accountant as also the Auditor; whose services are at the pleasure of this employer whom he is supposed to be auditing. The Auditor, more or less, becomes a collaborator in the process of concealing, rather than exposing which should be his primary job. In India, by and large, he becomes a conspirator by virtue of the infrastructural arrangement in which he has to work. It is he who aids and abets to evade taxes and conspires to hide black money. If it were not possible to hide, the generation of black money itself would stop or at least slow down considerably.

Like other professions, this one is also tightly held in our medieval dwarf mindset. This soulless functioning needs to be checked. The following suggestions could be useful in our context.

(a) Audit & Accounting be completely separated i.e. auditing & accounting firms should be different. Select persons/ firms be given the certificate for audit and they should not be allowed to do accounting and those with accounting practice should be barred from auditing.

(b) Emoluments of an auditor/accountant be determined by some Association of Auditors/Accountants or some government agency or some other independent agency.

(c) The auditors should not be picked up by the corporates / individuals themselves but by some central professional authority constituted for the purpose and this very body should pay them and not the firm/corporate being audited so as to free them from any control or tail twisting by the corporates/individuals. It is a different matter that the money paid will have to be recovered from this firm only, but there would be no direct *quid pro quo* between the auditor and the subject being audited.

(d) If an auditor is not acceptable to the firm/individual being audited, reasons be conveyed in writing. These reasons will be thoroughly examined by the authority and if justified then only the change could be made, but under no circumstance will the auditor be his nominee.

The USA learnt great lessons out of Enron as is apparent from the quote below from Alan Greenpan, Chairman, US Federal Reserve, "Even though Enron was a great tragedy for a number of people, especially the employees who worked there, it probably has created a positive set of forces to improve corporate governance. I think we are going to find it was a net plus to our economy."

How true it is in our context today, but despite a number of mishaps, with Satyam the latest and perhaps the biggest, we have done nothing practically. We need strengthen our systems and give soul to the professionals for meaningful results. In our country we fear and hesitate in cleansing our systems, but once we start working in cleaner atmosphere, we will realize what a great feeling it is.

Above are some of the measures that can be adopted by us. These are capable to usher in a revolutionary change and control generation of the black money itself. The greatest advantage to us as a nation, as a society and as a welfare state committed to amelioration of the conditions of its masses would be that the black money will decline and so also the Indian deposits abroad and we will progress fast.

8

Conclusion

Bringing back the black money is a long drawn out task that may take decades and still there would be uncertainty whether the money will actually come back or not. In any case chances appear to be rather bleak. We do not have the capacity to exert the sort of pressure the USA could and bend the Swiss banks. Moreover our ruling class, who fear being exposed, will never like to take any initiative. However, the middle and in particular the lower classes are getting restive. They have come to realize that it is their money. They have been duped and deprived through dubious means, of what rightfully is theirs and they have been thrown into the lap of poverty and misery that they did not deserve. A few years ago they hardly appreciated the huge implications, but the propaganda in recent elections has changed the perception and triggered their aspirations. If nothing is done it will slowly build up as a movement and cause havoc just like Naxalism. Young men, in particular, may take recourse to violence and that will pose very serious problems for peace and development of the country and also for those who possess such money/assets.

It is absolutely necessary that all out efforts be made to bring back our money stashed abroad even if we know that nothing will come out of it. People will feel convinced about the bonafides of the government. Even if the money does not come back, the step will prevent further siphoning abroad and improve tax collections. That would provide immediate relief to these impoverished classes and would also be a sort of insurance that at least no money would be drained out of the country in future.

The economy needs to be brought under the ambit of the law for which it is necessary that cash transactions be confined to the minimum and all the major transactions should be recorded and routed through the banking channels. It will be more prudent to take care of future as that part is in our own hands, though at the same time it is also absolutely necessary that we build all the pressure on our own and through the world forums so that at least part of the money comes back and more important that names along with accounting details of such persons can be obtained in order to take action against them inland as opening an account abroad is not permissible without authority from the Reserve Bank of India. Further, such information may lead to link their investments in the form of FDI or otherwise in the country and abroad.

From time to time useful suggestions have been made, but the Indian state in the hands of perpetrators of black money never acted on them. As early as 1951 Gorwala had suggested: "In the state of our laws it may not be possible to hang influential black-marketeers and tax-evaders from the lamp posts, but it is certainly within every minister's capacity not to consult them, to show them no favour, to avoid having social contact with them, to refuse to make speeches at gatherings where they take a leading part or to accept purses from them." But Gorwala was not heeded and all these activities continued unabated and the biggest financial supporters of our politicians in elections are deep into all the above vices.

As early as 1964, the Santhanam Committee on Corruption in order to impart punch to the provisions of law dealing with black money had listed the following offences with the observations to class them as the substantive offences on the lines of offences against human body or the property as these "....social offences having regard to the special circumstances under which they are committed, and which have now become a dominant feature of certain powerful sections of modern society". The offences are:

1. Offences calculated to prevent or obstruct the economic development of the country and endanger its economic health;
2. Evasion and avoidance of taxes lawfully imposed;
3. Misuse of their position by public servants in making of contracts and disposal of public property, issue of licenses and permits and similar other matters;
4. Delivery by individuals and industrial and commercial undertakings of goods not in accordance with agreed specifications in fulfilment of contracts entered into with public authorities;
5. Profiteering, black-marketing and hoarding;
6. Adulteration of foodstuffs and drugs;
7. Theft and misappropriation of public property and funds; and
8. Trafficking in licenses, permits, etc.

The Committee is correct that all these offences are taken very lightly in law though these are of fundamental importance to the economy and the social health of the country. People who matter may publicly shout for upliftment of the poor or of hanging the blackmarketeer from the nearest lamp post that we have been hearing ever since the independence, but the fact is that no laws have been provided any punch. On the contrary if some such law happened to possess some teeth that was dropped from the statute book. The deterrence that a law is supposed to provide, has systematically been eroded. Replacement of FERA by FEMA is one such Act. FEMA is practically a civil violation and not a criminal offence. When we approach Swiss banks, the possible reasons for getting back our money can be :

(a) It is the money involved in crime of corruption, terrorism or drugs.

(b) The money is born out of any other crime relating to foreign exchanges or the tax evasion.

We do not have registered cases along with the requisite standard of evidence so far as substantive crime under category "a" above is concerned and the category "b" is not defined as crime even in India. *Prima facie* we face an uphill task in bringing back the money.

However, the country expects action from the Prime Minister who is revered as an economist, an academician and an honest person though surrounded by dishonest and fraudulent crowds, by and large, who themselves may be having such accounts like any other person in power in India. It may be argued that if action is taken, the government may fall as most of the elites including the civil servants and big businessmen also hold such slush. The moot point is whether the PM owes his loyalty to such criminals or to the nation. What if the government of the day falls, the nation will surely rise? The nation will be galvanized, will be hopeful about future and the PM would have an occasion to select a more honest team. The PM is fortunate to be blessed with this great opportunity, but if he ignores or misses it, he will be answerable to the nation, to himself and to the history. Such tailor-made opportunities seldom visit though only the brave can avail. One can extend best wishes and cooperation to the PM if he undertakes this most sacrosanct national task.

Black money is a national problem. The issue needs not be dragged into political controversy and allowed to be killed. As pointed out earlier all the political parties and the politicians of all shades are responsible for it. The politician cannot cast away his responsibility as he is the leader of the show chosen by the people. If he choses to avoid this problem for another decade, the whole country may plunge into the far more serious problems including Naxalism as also may land in the lap of other disruptive forces. No nation can afford to exploit the majority of population like that. During the last 20 years the number of districts in the fold of Naxalism has gone up from a single digit to a high three digits. We cannot afford to let it rise anymore and nor can such a campaign related to exploitation can be contained by police or any other force. Coercion may appear to contain it, but the reprieve will be temporary only. Indiscriminate violence indulged into by the Naxalites is condemnable, but their ideology of *Roti, Kapda aur Makan* to all, is absolutely pious and relevant where more than 50 percent of people live on less than half a dollar a day. The force may only quell some targeted Naxalites, but not the Naxalism as more and more of hungry, exploited people will keep on rising in revolt. They have deliverance by dying rather than living a life of serfdom, exploitation and hunger. The basic rationale that is intimately linked to black money, has to be addressed, as in this age of growing awareness, the problem is staring hard in our face. If not tackled on economic plain by the politician, the people would tackle it through revolution, but that will be a very destructive path for which the responsibility will lie on those who did not act appropritely in time.

It may be added here that conditions are worsening as a committe of the Planning Commission has recently reported that 78 per cent of population live on less than Rs. 20 a day. Suresh Tendulkar committe that submitted its reports in second week of December 2009 has not been made public as yet, but some highlights have appeared in print media that place the percentage of people below poverty line at 37.2 per cent, a huge raise of 15.6 over 21.6 per cent as reported in the Economic Survey 2008-2009 presented in the Union Parliament by the union finance minister. Without access to the report it can be safely inferred that the tax evasion and the generation of black money are on the rise and the rich and influential section of the society are poaching hard on the share of the poor and the downtrodden.

Allout efforts need be made to combat the black income and also to collect taxes. Discontinuation of higher denomination notes has become a pre-requisite. This can be the starting point of our effective constructive action. If the due taxes to the extent of Rs. 30 lac crores per annum are collected in the country, there should be no shortage of funds for creation of infrastructure like roads, provision of water, electricity or for providing foolproof defences to the country. Besides providing services like education, health, water, sanitation, out of this collection without entailing any further cess or depriving the lower sections down the line of these services that only make the life worth living. The only loss would be to the extra luxurious life style for those who are indulging in black money. That may cut down the number of Mercedes and BMWs (that are brought in the country mostly evading various duties) i.e. all that they can't explain through fair means. Further, curbing of black money will reduce the gap between the rich and the poor without any subsidy or pity. Also, there would be no need for bleeding the country through mechanism of BOT for roads or the flyovers, as State will have enough to invest on creation of the required infrastructures without recourse to the begging bowl.

Annexure A

Countries that have Tax Havens

GLOBAL POLICY FORUM
777 UN Plaza, Suite 3D
New York, NY 10017 USA
Phone +1 212 557 3161
Fax +1 212 557 3165

Following is the table of countries that are on the respective lists of these organisations.

	OECD	U.S. Stop Tax Havens Abuse Act	IMF	Tax Research Org
ANDORRA	un-cooperative	no	yes	yes
ANGUILLA	cooperative	yes	yes	yes
ANTIGUA AND BARBUDA	cooperative	yes	yes	yes
ARUBA	cooperative	yes	yes	yes
BAHAMAS	cooperative	yes	yes	yes
BARBADOS	no	yes	yes	yes
BAHRAIN	cooperative	no	yes	yes
BELIZE	cooperative	yes	yes	yes
BERMUDA	cooperative	yes	yes	yes
BOTSWANA	no	no	yes	no
BRITISH VIRGIN ISLANDS	cooperative	yes	yes	yes
BRUNEI	no	no	yes	no
CAPE VERDE	no	no	yes	no

Contd...

CAYMAN ISLANDS	cooperative	yes	yes	yes
COOK ISLANDS	cooperative	yes	yes	yes
COSTA RICA	no	yes	yes	yes
CYPRUS	cooperative	yes	yes	yes
DOMINICA	cooperative	yes	yes	yes
DUBAI	no	no	yes	no
GIBRALTAR	cooperative	yes	yes	yes
GRENADA	cooperative	yes	yes	yes
GUERNSEY	cooperative	yes *	yes	yes
HONG KONG	no	yes	yes	yes
ISLE OF MAN	cooperative	yes	yes	yes
IRELAND	no	no	yes	yes
JERSEY	cooperative	yes	yes	yes
LATVIA	no	yes	no	no
LEBANON	no	no	yes	yes
LIBERIA	cooperative	no	no	yes
LIECHTENSTEIN	un-cooperative	yes	yes	yes
LUXEMBOURG	no	yes	yes	yes
MACAU	no	no	yes	yes
MALAYSIA (LABUAN)	no	no	yes	yes
MALDIVES	no	no	no	yes
MALTA	cooperative	yes	yes	yes
MARSHALL ISLANDS	cooperative	no	yes	yes
MAURITIUS	cooperative	no	yes	yes
MONACO	un-cooperative	no	yes	yes
MONTSERRAT	cooperative	no	yes	yes
NAURU	cooperative	yes	yes	yes
NETHERLANDS ANTILLES	cooperative	yes	yes	yes
NIUE	ooperative	no	yes	yes
PALAU	no	no	yes	no
PANAMA	cooperative	yes	yes	yes
SAMOA	cooperative	yes	yes	yes

Contd...

SAN MARINO	cooperative	no	yes	no
SEYCHELLES	cooperative	no	yes	yes
SINGAPORE	no	yes	yes	yes
ST. KITTS & NEVIS	cooperative	yes	yes	yes
ST. LUCIA	cooperative	yes	yes	yes
ST. VINCENT				
AND THE GRENADINES	cooperative	yes	yes	yes
SWITZERLAND	no	yes	yes	yes
TURKS & CAICOS ISLANDS	cooperative	yes	yes	yes
UNITED KINGDOM	no	no	no	yes
URUGUAY	no	no	yes	no
U.S. VIRGIN ISLANDS	cooperative	no	no	no
VANUATU	cooperative	yes	yes	yes
* (includes Sark/Alderney)				
yes = country is on the list				
no = country is not on the list				
(Reporting by Douwe Miedema)				

Note from the author:

Above is the list of the counties that have tax havens. Some of these have more than one such institutions as Cayman Island has 8–the highest number, followed by Antigua & Barbua and Nauru–7 each, Bahrain–6 and Brunei 5. So the total number is much higher than the number of countries recounted above.

Annexure B

Word Copy of Satyendra K. Dubey Letter to PM of October 11, 2002

(...but in reality a great loot of public money...
Satyendra K. Dubey)
In Rs. 56,000 crores NHAI Projects

http://www.indianexpress.com/res/web/ple full
story.php?content_id=36695

To

The Prime Minister
Republic of India
Prime Minister's Office
New Delhi - 110 001

Sub: National Highways Development Project (Golden Quadrilateral and North-South, East-West Corridors) —

A dream project of unparalleled importance to the Nation ***but in reality a great loot of public money because of very poor implementation at every state.***

Hon'ble Sir,

Through this letter, I wish to draw your kind attention towards great lapse in the implementation of above project. Since such letters from a common man are not usually treated with due seriousness, I wish to clarify at the outset that this letter is being written after careful thought by a very concerned citizen of the country who is also very closely linked with the project. I request you to kindly go through my brief particulars (attached on a separate sheet to ensure secrecy) before proceeding further.

Instead of writing at length, I would be very specific and to the point highlighting the areas where there have been great lapses and would suggest certain remedies to the best of my abilities. I have been posted both at NHAI, HQ and at site on NH-2 Projects and therefore my direct experience is with NH-2 Projects (World Bank Funded). However, the story is almost same with all other projects which are under implementation and would be no different for forthcoming Projects unless we take certain corrective measures immediately. **I have gone through most of the files (even closed ones) dealing with NH-2 projects (their design consultancy, procurement of civil contractors, selection of supervision consultants, the mobilisation of contractors. and consultants, etc.). The areas of concern are highlighted below:**

Preparation of Detail Project Reports (DPRs) by the Design Consultants

The DPRs prepared by the design consultants are **in very poor shape and cannot be implemented in the field without major modifications**. It appears that the design consultants have made the designs and drawings with little consideration for the actual ground conditions and the same have been accepted by NHAI without any scrutiny. The proof consultants (deployed for checking DPRs, submitted by Design Consultants) appear to have done only cosmetic work and it appears that the officers in NHAI have not even opened the final DPRs submitted by the consultants before putting the works to tender. The result is that the DPRs, on the basis of which tenders have been called, are like garbage. When the problems are being noticed in DPR at the implementation stage and the design consultants are being requested to clarify them, we are getting a cold and negative response from them. This is contributing to delay in the implementation of projects.

A good DPR is one of the foremost requirements for the smooth implementation of the project and we are faltering at the very initial stage. In the present system there appears to be no accountability on the part of design consultant. To ensure this, we should evolve a system whereby the design consultant can be made accountable for any problem in the implementation of DPR and their consequent implications in terms of time and cost overruns. A system of insurance may be devised to address this issue. The design consultant may be asked to keep his establishment at site in the initial stage of implementation of project, so that any design issue may be addressed speedily. Alternatively, we may link substantial portion of payment of design consultants to the implementation of DPR in the field. Another way may be to award design consultancy (for preparation of DPR) and supervision consultancy (to supervise the execution of project) to the same consultancy firm so that any discrepancy noticed in DPR at the execution stage is corrected by the same firm. We may deliberate further to arrive at the most suitable option.

Procurement of Civil Contractors

The process of procurement appears to have been completely manipulated and hijacked by the big contractors. Many contractors are submitting forged documents to justify their technical and financial capabilities to execute the project. The big contractors have been able to get all sorts of help (including even the most secret information and documents) from the officials in NHAI and even the note sheets carrying approval of chairman have been leaked outside. (This mostly appears to have been done by lower officials and supporting staff). **Little thought has been given to the ability and sincerity of some of the contractors to do the work they have quoted for. The three striking examples are awards of NH-2 to M/s Centrodors toy of Russia, M/s China Coal of China and M/s LG of South Korea which are all working like commission agents by collaborating with local incompetent and inexperienced firms and trying to get the work done through**

them. M/s Progressive Constructions Ltd is another contractor which appears to have completely manipulated the system to get the award of 2 projects on NH-2. This company is not organised on professional lines and it is run like a family business. They get one work and assign it to one relative, the second is assigned to another and the story goes on.

There is an urgent need to have a fresh look at the whole procurement process and utmost care needs to be exercised at the time of selection of contractors. The whole process should be made more transparent and any official found colluding with the contractors should be severely punished.

Mobilisation of Contractors and Mobilisation Advance to them

NHAI officials have shown great hurry in giving mobilisation advance to the selected contractors (**no surprise, as the commission to officials for award of work are linked to the contractors getting their first mobilisation advance**). In some cases the contractors have been given mobilisation advance just a day after signing the Contract Agreement. The entire mobilisation advance of 10 per cent of contract value (**which goes up to Rs. 40 crores in certain cases**) has been paid to the contractors within a few weeks of award of work but there has been little follow-up to ensure that they are actually mobilised at site with the same pace. The result is that the entire mobilisation advance remains lying with contractors (or get diverted in their other activities) for months — a way for contractors to make easy money and for client to loose interest charges on them. **Most of the contractors have not mobilised even up to 50 per cent a year after getting their mobilisation advances.**

Similar diversion or idling of funds are taking place in case of equipment advances to the contractors, **another 10 per cent of the contract value.** In many cases, the equipment is not being purchased and, even if purchased, is being used somewhere else. The contractors are getting customs and excise duty exemptions on most of the road construction equipment. However, because of laxity on the part of NHAI, the contractors in many cases are buying equipment on behalf of **or for other parties and appropriating a portion of the excise/custom duty exemptions in their pocket.**

We need to be vigilant and careful in giving advances to the contractors. The advances are given to the contractors to mobilise them quickly in the interest of project and therefore the same should be linked to their actual mobilisation at site. **The advances should be given in instalments and the release of next instalment** should be made dependent on utilisation of the previous instalment. A strict vigil and audit needs to be done to ensure that the advances are used by contractors for quick mobilisation and are utilised in the same project for which they are being given.

Selection of Supervision Consultants and Design Consultants

The concept of supervision consultancy is a step in very right direction and the amount spent on them (**roughly 2-3 percent of the cost of civil works**) is a good investment. But here again we are faltering at the implementation stage.

There is **a big fraud in the selection of Supervision/Design consultants** which mainly depends on their technical manpower. To get the consultancy work, the consultants are proposing to deploy well-qualified and senior professionals in their **technical proposals (many times their qualification and experience are being forged and NHAI officials are not taking any pain to ask for the documentary proof** in support of their claims).

Many a time, the same professional figures simultaneously in technical proposals forwarded by many consultants and NHAI officials are doing little to discourage it. However, once that work is awarded to them, they are invariably coming with the request for replacement of their proposed personnel with professionals of much less qualification and experience.

To our shame, we in NHAI are giving least resistance to this trend and the proposals for replacement of professionals are being approved freely. The curriculum vitae of professionals are invariably being fabricated and manipulated by consultants to get approval, as the NHAI officials are not asking for any documentary proof in support of the qualification and experience claimed. Instead they are abetting this crime.

The consultants in first instance come with the replacement CV to have an informal discussion with the officials. However, once they are given the feeling that the same can't be approved on file, the CV of same man is properly fabricated (in connivance with NHAI officials) and submitted formally and the approval is granted. This is the state of affairs.

The end result is that the consultants propose to deploy the most qualified, experienced and senior men in their organisation (or outside their organisation) to get the work and, once awarded the work, replace them with much inferior persons. They propose the same senior team to get another work and repeat the same story of replacement and the drama goes on.

This way, the consultants are completely manipulating the system. The well-qualified persons in head offices of consultancy firms are thus being used simply to get the work, but they are not being sent to the site, where they are being proposed to be deployed. The field units of these consultancy firms are instead being asked by their head offices to look for the required personnel. The result is that many key professional posts are lying vacant for months or are being filled by unqualified person. In all these, it is the project which ultimately suffers.

This whole drama can be very easily checked provided we have the will. It is all the more easy in the totally computerised system at NHAI. A few steps outlined below will go a long way in remedying this ill.

1. No consultant should be allowed to propose the deployment of same professional in more than one technical proposal.
2. It should be ensured that the same person is not proposed to be deployed by more than one consultancy firm.

3. It should be ensured that the person proposed by a consultancy firm is actually working in the firm or is having a bond with the firm to work in the project if the firm is awarded the project.
4. Replacement should be approved only under very extraordinary circumstances and a penalty should be imposed on the firm for their inability to deploy the proposed professional.
5. All documentary proof in support of the qualification and experience claimed by a person should be asked.

In summary, it should be ensured that the supervision consultants deploy a well qualified and experienced team for proper supervision of the work. This becomes all the more important, because the supervision consultant (known as Engineer in FIDIC contract document) has been given immense powers and responsibilities under FIDIC conditions of contract which we are following.

The Problem of Subletting or Subcontracting

The NHAI is going for International Competitive Bidding to procure the most competent Civil Contractor for execution of its projects. The works are usually being awarded at high cost and the contractors are assuring the best quality in the execution of projects. **However, when it comes to the actual execution of works, it is found that most of the works (sometimes even up to 100 per cent) are being sublet or subcontracted to small petty contractors who are not at all capable to execute such big projects and ensure the quality of construction assured by the Civil Contractors** As a result, the entire process of shortlisting and pre-qualification of contractors and international competitive bidding are being nullified and what we are getting are the numerous petty contractors working at site and making a mockery of the prestigious project. The main Civil Contractors who have been awarded the work by NHAI are doing all these under the veil of labour contract which is permissible under the contract agreement. But in reality, they are getting most of the work done through numerous small petty contractors (main contractors are supplying only a few critical equipment and materials) at 50-60 per cent of the price quoted by them **and the rest 40 per cent of contract price is being pocketed by them without much effort. In the process, the main contractors. are working just like commission agents.**

I would like to mention here that the above phenomena of subletting and subcontracting is **known to all from top to bottom but every one is maintaining a studied silence**. It would not be inappropriate to say that all these mouths have been shut by these big contractors who are manipulating the system and individuals alike. These petty contractors are bringing poor equipment and material, giving a big setback to the progress and quality of work. The main contractors are least bothered about the timely completion of projects (and penalties, if they are unable to finish the work in time) as they are quite sure of getting time extension by manipulating the individuals. They have already started fabricating spurious claims to make grounds for time extension and cost overruns. If this issue of subcontracting is not taken up with urgency, the entire project will be a very big failure both in terms of quality of construction and timely completion.

This issue cannot be expected to be tackled by field units of NHAI as the decision to sublet the works are being taken by head offices of the contractors and not their field units. To address this, the top administration in NHAI has to take up the matter aggressively with the top management of contractors.

NHAI Organisation and office system

It would not be inappropriate to say that there is no system in NHAI, there are only individuals. There is an urgent need to review and restructure the office procedure and office set up including the file system. Record keeping is very poor and it would be difficult to trace even the most important papers after sometime.

The entire organisation is almost based on sourcing people on deputation basis. There is a need to have some permanent cadre strength in NHAI. In its zeal to maintain a lean and thin organisation, one accounts officer/manager (finance) is allotted to two Project Implementation units spaced around 200-300 km apart, which is a mere nonsense. There is an immediate need to deploy one accounts officer/manager (finance) in each PIU, which manage projects of around Rs.1,000 crores.

The earlier we take up these issues, the better it is for the health of NHAI. If some well-planned measures are not taken soon, the NHAI as a system is headed for a big failure.

As a concerned citizen of the country, I have brought these issues to your notice for your kind intervention and necessary action. Looking at the enormity of public fund involved in the project, the matter needs your urgent attention.

I have written all these in my individual capacity. However, I will keep on addressing these issues in my official capacity in the limited domain within the powers delegated to me. If any elaboration/clarification is needed on above issues, I would be glad to render all my assistance in the interest of this very prestigious National Highways Development Project, which is undoubtedly the biggest ever project undertaken in India after independence.

Thanking you

Yours sincerely

Annexure C

Don't Handover Dharavi on a Platter for a Song-II

Maharashtra Government has at last finalized a scheme for upliftment of Dharavi, the biggest slum spread over an area of 557 acres. Dharavi is situated in the heart of Mumbai and if developed on modern lines, it will command a very high price equivalent to any posh area in the city. According to the press reports, the plan as formulated envisages construction of structures covering a floor area seven crore square feet, of which two crore sft will be given to the present dwellers who are occupying the sprawling slums. This will also include the area required for common facilities like school, hospitals etc. It will leave out an area of 5 crores sft with the private builders for consideration of constructing the 2 crore sft of space. They can develop the rest and dispose it off, as they like. It sounds quite good *prima facie* that the slum dwellers will get pucca houses free of cost, but reality is equally deceptive and sordid as that will set a very dangerous trend and precedent and create new and strengthen the old land and builders' mafias in Mumbai. It appears either the powers to be have colluded with the construction lobby or the authorities are too naive to appreciate the implications of this deal as the following analysis in a little depth will bring home the naked sellout that the deal in fact is.

The accommodation meant for slum dwellers is proposed to consist of the basic multi-storeyed small flats covering 224 sft per unit only. The specifications will naturally be of the lowest level. The cost of construction would be very low. At present rates, it may not exceed Rs. 800/- per sft. But even if we take it Rs. 1000/- per sft, the cost of construction for 2 crore sft works out to Rs. 2000 crore only. Thus the private sector, all combined, will spend Rs. 2000 crore and will get the remaining land. Since the FAR is constant that means the land for the slum dwellers and the builders will be divided in a ratio of 2:5 or 160 acres for the slum dwellers and 400 acres for the builders for a consideration of Rs. 2000 crore or Rs. 5 crore an acre. That is no price for Mumbai as sometime back the NTC land similarly situated had fetched Rs. 1.53 lac to Rs. 4 lac per sq.yd or Rs. 74 crores to 193 crores per acre. Taking the middle or the average figure of Rs. 133.5 crores per acre, the total works out to Rs. 53400 crores much for the raw land at the most depressed price level.

Looking from the point of view of constructed area, which is more realistic, the implications soar high exponentially. Even in the ordinary areas the prevailing rate as given in media is placed at 17,000 per sft or Rs. 85000 crores for the rest of five crores sft., whereas this land is situated in the heart of Mumbai. The other day in the posh area a residential flat was sold @97400 per sft. At that rate the built up area in the present case would work out to Rs. 487000 crore. If even half the floor area out of the 5 crore sft is developed as posh, it would still earn a whopping Rs. 2.43 lac crore, in addition to Rs 42500 crores that the ordinary half would earn. Further part of it is supposed to be commercial, which commands astronomical rates in this metropolis. Sometime back a TV programme cited a rate of Rs. 5 lacs per sft. There is no doubt that the total returns are sure to be over Rs. 5 lac crore. Against a cost of construction for the superior quality is not going to exceed Rs. 2000 per sft or a total of Rs. 10000 crores. Adding the cost of construction for the slum dwellers; on an investment of Rs. 12000 crore, the bounty would be almost Rs. 5 lac crores. Why the state is showing such a great generosity to the mafia. Assuming there are no bad intentions, then the arithmetic need be learnt and corrected; but God forbid if intentions are not honourable, then it is a sell out of the nation, that will create huge black money enough to submerge the economy of Mumbai widen the gap between the rich and the poor, push up the price level and the resultant inflation and loot the people down the line as also the state exchequer.

No wonder all the big industrial and business houses are reported to be running for getting this prime land. If later on some raise is managed in the FAR the margins will go up further, the State or the people will only get a token of the floor area free. If the state means business, not more than 50 lac sft should be given to the builder for building the remaining 6.5 crore sft free of cost, otherwise the state can construct on its own, as it has requisite apparatus and it can engage the private sector not as builder but as contractor on the competitive rates.

There is another aspect to it, that the slum dwellers are being cheated by allowing them a small area of 224 sft only, which does not constitute a house. It is well known that builders talk of the super area that includes the space occupied by walls, the staircase, the corridors etc, that take away 35 percent of the super area leaving out only 145 sft. A toilet, a bath and a kitchen require a minimum of 60 sft. That leaves the room size as small as 85 sft. as against the minimum room size of 100 sft for human living as per any architectural norms. When they are surrendering such a sprawling land mass that they have occupied for so long, why they don't have a title to a livable house covering a floor area of 600 sft that can give them two rooms with other necessary accessories. They deserve that and should be provided with accommodation which is worth living, instead of bundling and huddling the whole family together like cattle in just one small dingy 85 sft hole, where there is no place for movement, no privacy and no space for children to study. In such small accommodation the children acquire a very constricted outlook. Let us save this big chunk of our next generation from such a catastrophe and think of the welfare of the owners of this land. Though it is their right but still they are paying for generosity and consideration, which should not be overlooked in a civilized country, boasting of being a welfare state.

Annexure D

Tax to GDP Ratio

Country	Per cent	Per cent	Per cent
Afghanistan	6.4		
Albania	22.9		
Algeria	7.7		
Angola	5.7		
Argentina	22.9		
Armenia	14.1		
Australia	30.5	30.6	
Austria	43.4	41.9	41.8
Azerbaijan	17.8		
Bahamas, The	18.7		
Bahrain	2.4		
Bangladesh	8.5		
Barbados	32.6		
Belarus	24.2		
Belgium	46.8	44.4	44.6
Belize	21.6		
Benin	15.4		

Contd...

Bhutan	10.7		
Bolivia	27.0		
Bosnia and Herzegovina	41.2		
Botswana	35.2		
Brazil	38.8		
Bulgaria	34.4		34.4
Burkina Faso	11.5		
Burma	4.9		
Burundi	17.4		
Cambodia	8.0		
Cameroon	18.2		
Canada	33.4	33.3	
Cape Verde	23.0		
Central African Republic	7.7		
Chad	4.2		
Chile	17.1		
China, People's Republic of	17.0		
China, Republic of (Taiwan)	12.4		
Colombia	23.0		
Comoros	12.0		
Congo, Republic of	5.9		
Costa Rica	14.0		
Côte d'Ivoire	15.3		
Croatia	26.6		
Cuba	44.8		
Cyprus	36.6		36.6

Contd...

Czech Republic	36.3	36.4	36.2
Denmark	50.0	48.9	49.1
Djibouti	20.0		
Dominica	30.3		
Dominican Republic	15.0		
Congo, Democratic Republic of	13.2		
Ecuador	13.2		
Egypt	15.8		
El Salvador	13.3		
Equatorial Guinea	1.7		
Estonia	31.1		31.0
Ethiopia	11.6		
Fiji	21.8		
Finland	43.6	43.0	43.5
France	46.1	43.6	44.2
Gabon	10.3		
Gambia	18.9		
Georgia	21.7		
Germany	40.6	36.2	39.3
Ghana	20.8		
Greece	33.5	31.3	31.4
Guatemala	11.9		
Guinea	8.2		
Guinea-Bissau	11.5		
Guyana	31.9		
Haiti	9.4		

Contd...

Honduras	15.6		
Hong Kong	12.8		
Hungary	37.3	39.3	37.2
Iceland	40.4	41.4	
India	17.7		
Indonesia	11.0		
Iran	7.3		
Ireland	34.0	32.2	32.6
Israel	36.8		
Italy	42.6	43.3	42.3
Jamaica	27.2		
Japan	27.4	27.9	
Jordan	21.1		
Kazakhstan	26.8		
Kenya	18.4		
Kiribati	91.6		
Korea, South	26.8	28.7	
Kuwait	1.5		
Kyrgyzstan	21.4		
Laos	10.8		
Latvia	30.4		30.1
Lebanon	14.4		
Lesotho	42.9		
Liberia	13.2		
Libya	2.7		
Lithuania	20.9		29.7

Contd...

Luxembourg	36.4	36.9	35.6
Macau	20.1		
Macedonia	29.3		
Madagascar	10.7		
Malawi	20.7		
Malaysia	15.5		
Maldives	20.5		
Mali	15.3		
Malta	35.2		33.8
Mauritania	15.4		
Mauritius	18.1		
Mexico	9.7	20.5	
Micronesia	12.3		
Moldova	33.8		
Mongolia	33.8		
Montenegro	28.0		
Morocco	22.3		
Mozambique	13.4		
Namibia	28.8		
Nepal	10.9		
Netherlands	39.5	38.0	39.5
New Zealand	36.5	36.0	
Nicaragua	17.8		
Niger	11.0		
Nigeria	6.1		
Norway	43.6	43.4	44.0

Contd...

Oman	2.0		
Pakistan	10.6		
Panama	10.6		
Papua New Guinea	24.5		
Paraguay	12.0		
Peru	15.1		
Philippines	14.4		
Poland	33.8	33.5	33.8
Portugal	37.0	36.6	35.9
Qatar	2.2		
Romania	28.1		28.6
Russia	36.9		
Rwanda	14.1		
Saint Lucia	23.1		
Saint Vincent and the Grenadines	26.5		
Samoa	25.5		
Sao Tome and Principe	17.4		
Saudi Arabia	5.3		
Senegal	19.2		
Serbia	34.1		
Seychelles	32.0		
Sierra Leone	10.5		
Singapore	13.0		
Slovakia	29.5	29.8	29.3
Slovenia	39.3		39.1
Solomon Islands	24.7		

Contd...

South Africa	26.9		
Spain	37.3	37.2	36.5
Sri Lanka	15.3		
Sudan	6.3		
Suriname/Surinam	22.1		
Swaziland	39.8		
Sweden	49.7	48.2	48.9
Switzerland	30.1	29.7	
Syria	10.7		
Tajikistan	16.5		
Tanzania	12.0		
Thailand	17.0		
Timor-Leste	109.7		
Togo	15.5		
Tonga	27.0		
Trinidad and Tobago	28.0		
Tunisia	14.9		
Turkey	32.5	23.7	
Turkmenistan	20.2		
Uganda	12.6		
Ukraine	38.1		
United Arab Emirates	1.4		
United Kingdom	39.0	36.6	37.4
United States	28.2	28.3	
Uruguay	23.1		
Uzbekistan	21.0		

Contd...

Vanuatu	17.8		
Venezuela	25.0		
Vietnam	13.8		
Yemen	7.1		
Zambia	16.1		
Zimbabwe	49.3		

Annexure E

Extracts from UN Convention Against Corruption – 2003

Article 6: Preventive Anti-corruption Body or Bodies

1. Each State Party shall, in accordance with the fundamental principles of its legal system, ensure the existence of a body or bodies, as appropriate, that prevent corruption ......
2. Each State Party shall grant the body or bodies referred to in paragraph 1 of this article the necessary independence, in accordance with the fundamental principles of its legal system, to enable the body or bodies to carry out its or their functions effectively and free from any undue influence.

Article 11(2)

Measures to the same effect as those taken pursuant to paragraph 1 of this article may be introduced and applied within the prosecution service in those State Parties where it does not form part of the judiciary but enjoys independence similar to that of the judicial service.

Article 36: Specialized Authorities

Each State Party shall, in accordance with the fundamental principles of its legal system, ensure the existence of a body or bodies or persons specialized in combating corruption through law enforcement. Such body or bodies or pers.ons shall be granted the necessary independence, in accordance with the fundamental principles of the legal system of the State Party, to be able to carry out their functions effectively and without any undue influence

Article 40: Bank Secrecy

Each State Party shall ensure that, in the case of domestic criminal investigations of offences established in accordance with this Convention, there are appropriate mechanisms available within its domestic legal system to overcome obstacles that may arise out of the application of bank secrecy laws.

Article 43: International Cooperation

1. State Parties shall cooperate in criminal matters in accordance with articles 44 to 50 of this Convention. Where appropriate and consistent with their domestic legal system, State Parties shall consider assisting each other in investigations of and proceedings in civil and administrative matters relating to corruption.
2. In matters of international cooperation, whenever dual criminality is considered a requirement, it shall be deemed fulfilled irrespective of whether the laws of the requested State Party place the offence within the same category of offence or denominate the offence by the same terminology as the requesting State Party, if the conduct underlying the offence for which assistance is sought is a criminal offence under the laws of both State Parties.
8. State Parties shall not decline to render mutual legal assistance pursuant to this article on the ground of bank secrecy.
9. *(a)* A requested State Party, in responding to a request for assistance pursuant to this article in the absence of dual criminality, shall take into account the purposes of this Convention, as set forth in article 1.

Index

Some of our learned Authors

General S Padmanabhan; General VP Malik; Admiral Vishnu Bhagwat; Dr A Sivathanu Pillai, DRDO; Parvez Dewan, IAS; Dhirendra Singh, IAS; Falguni Rajkumar, IAS; G Sundaram, IAS; PS Bhatnagar, IAS; N Vittal, IAS; PK Agrawal, IAS; Sudhir S Baloeria, IAS; NS Sisodia, IAS; Dr Yogendra Narain, IPS; J.K. Bagchi, IAS; TSR Subramanian, IAS; Air Chief Marshal FH Major, Prakash Singh, IPS; DC Nath, IPS; Ajit Doval, IPS; SP Mathur, IPS; Maloy Krishna Dhar, IPS; BR Lall, IPS; PC Dogra, IPS; DC Pathak, IPS; ML Kumawat, IPS; Dr. S Subramanian, IPS; RK Ohri, IPS; RB Sreekumar, IPS; Kalyan K Mitra, IPS; RS Gupta, IPS; K Koshy, IPS; Kuldeep Khoda, IPS; Ajay Kashyap, IPS; Dr N Dilip Kumar, IPS; Dr Nazrul Islam, IPS; Dr DV Guruprasad, IPS; AP Maheshwari, IPS; Loknath Behera, IPS; Dr NC Asthana, IPS; PM Nair, IPS; Dr Sundari Nanda, IPS; Keshav Kumar, IPS; Dr Prateep V Philip, IPS; Muktesh Chander, IPS; VK Agarwal, IRS; Virendra Gupta, IFS; Lt Gen SK Sinha; Lt. Gen Raj Kadyan; Lt Gen Mukesh Sabharwal; Lt Gen HB Kala; Lt Gen PC Katoch; Lt Gen Gautam Banerjee; Vice Admiral Suresh Bangara; Vice Admiral Vijay Shankar; Lt Gen Arjun Ray; Lt Gen CK Kapur; Lt Gen NS Narahari; Lt Gen Chandra Shekhar; Lt Gen ML Chibber; Lt Gen Ashok Joshi; Maj Gen Nilendra Kumar; Maj Gen Vinod Saighal; Maj Gen VK Singh; Maj Gen Anjan Mukherjee; Maj Gen Raj Mehta; Maj Gen Samay Ram; Maj Gen Dipankar Banerjee; Maj Gen Y Behl; Air Cmde RV Kumar; Air Marshal SR Deshpande; Air Marshal RC Bajpai; Air Vice Marshal AK Tiwary; Air Vice Marshal Samir K Sen; Air Cmde (Dr) CN Ghosh; Air Cmde NB Singh; Air Cmde RV Phadke; Arvind Gupta, IFS; Ambassador Kishan S Rana, IFS; Cmde Ranjit B Rai; Capt (IN) Alok Bansal; VK Singal, IRS; Sudha Raman; Brig Yash Mohan, VSM; Brig DK Khullar; Brig Trigunesh Mukherjee; Brig. (Dr.) HK Kar; Brig. MS Patil; Brig. Parmodh Sarin; Brig. RP Singh; Brig. Jaspal Singh; Col PK Gautam; Col MN Gulati; Col MS Jaswal; Col Anil Shorey; Lt Col Anil Bhatt; Dr RK Tiwari; Anuj Dhar, Journalist; Prakash Nanda, Journalist; Ranjit Kumar; Vijay Naik, Journalist and many more.